**New Directions for
Student Services**

Elizabeth J. Whitt
EDITOR-IN-CHIEF

John H. Schuh
ASSOCIATE EDITOR

Positive Psychology and Appreciative Inquiry in Higher Education

Peter C. Mather
Eileen Hulme
EDITORS

Number 143 • Fall 2013
Jossey-Bass
San Francisco

POSITIVE PSYCHOLOGY AND APPRECIATIVE INQUIRY IN HIGHER EDUCATION
Peter C. Mather, Eileen Hulme (eds.)
New Directions for Student Services, no. 143

Elizabeth J. Whitt, Editor-in-Chief
John H. Schuh, Associate Editor

NEW DIRECTIONS FOR STUDENT SERVICES (ISSN 0164-7970, e-ISSN 1536-0695) is part of The Jossey-Bass Higher and Adult Education Series and is published quarterly by Wiley Subscription Services, Inc., A Wiley Company, at Jossey-Bass, One Montgomery Street, Suite 1200, San Francisco, CA 94104-4594. POSTMASTER: Send address changes to New Directions for Student Services, Jossey-Bass, One Montgomery Street, Suite 1200, San Francisco, CA 94104-4594.

New Directions for Student Services is indexed in CIJE: Current Index to Journals in Education (ERIC), Contents Pages in Education (T&F), Current Abstracts (EBSCO), Education Index/Abstracts (H.W. Wilson), Educational Research Abstracts Online (T&F), ERIC Database (Education Resources Information Center), and Higher Education Abstracts (Claremont Graduate University).

Microfilm copies of issues and articles are available in 16mm and 35mm, as well as microfiche in 105mm, through University Microfilms Inc., 300 North Zeeb Road, Ann Arbor, Michigan 48106-1346.

SUBSCRIPTIONS cost $89 for individuals in the U.S., Canada, and Mexico, and $113 in the rest of the world for print only; $89 in all regions for electronic only; and $98 in the U.S., Canada, and Mexico for combined print and electronic; and $122 for combined print and electronic in the rest of the world. Institutional print only subscriptions are $311 in the U.S., $351 in Canada and Mexico, and $385 in the rest of the world; electronic only subscriptions are $311 in all regions; and combined print and electronic subscriptions are $357 in the U.S., $397 in Canada and Mexico, and $431 in the rest of the world.

EDITORIAL CORRESPONDENCE should be sent to the Editor-in-Chief, Elizabeth J. Whitt, University of California Merced, 5200 North Lake Rd. Merced, CA 95343.

www.josseybass.com

CONTENTS

EDITORS' NOTES

Positive psychology has received considerable attention from a variety of professional fields since its inception in the late 1990s. This movement marked a significant shift in the study of psychology from an emphasis on psychological deficits to scientific inquiry focused on aspects of human experiences that make life worth living.

Despite positive psychology's increasing prominence in areas such as business and public health, its influence on higher education has been modest, and is generally limited to the inclusion of "strengths assessment" in academic advising, first-year experience programming, and leadership education. The purpose of this monograph is to extend student affairs professionals' understanding of positive psychology's potential for supporting effective educational practice. The editors and authors of this volume represent practitioners and scholars who have investigated and applied this emerging scholarship to higher education and student affairs.

The connection between higher education and positive psychology is a natural one, as both are concerned with the formation of healthy, productive, and thriving human beings. Student affairs practitioners and scholars have historically sought to cultivate these outcomes through the application of human development theories. While student development theory provides a rich foundation for professional practice, we contend that it is valuable to supplement this theoretical lens with complementary approaches to enrich understanding of educational goals and processes.

Seligman (2002), the founder of the movement, has noted that there are three primary subjects of positive psychology: positive experiences (e.g., emotions), positive traits (e.g., strengths and engagement), and positive institutions. The contributors to this monograph explore all three of these dimensions. In addition, we have included appreciative inquiry (Cooperrider, Whitney, and Stavros, 2003), an organizational development method, as an important facet of positive practice. Although appreciative inquiry was conceived independently of positive psychology, these two areas share the foundational principles of improving practice through focusing on potential and the affirmation of what is working over the condemnation of what is not.

In his recent book, *Flourish,* Seligman (2011) identified five pillars of positive psychology: positive emotions, engagement, relationships, meaning, and accomplishment. These pillars denote "outcomes" associated with positive psychology research. As far back as Aristotle, philosophers and educators have examined and lauded the "good life" as a desirable educational outcome. These outcomes, we believe, are consonant with higher education and student affairs' rich history as well. On its face, we believe

NEW DIRECTIONS FOR STUDENT SERVICES, no. 143, Fall 2013 © Wiley Periodicals, Inc.
Published online in Wiley Online Library (wileyonlinelibrary.com) • DOI: 10.1002/ss.20054

that many higher education professionals will find resonance with positive psychology–related outcomes such as "optimal functioning" (Ryff and Singer, 2002) and "flourishing" (Keyes and Haidt, 2003; Seligman, 2011).

Positive psychology has been strengthened by its connection to seemingly disparate disciplines. With this in mind, this volume engages theories of leadership and organizational change, evolutionary psychology, and studies of spirituality, among others. We contend that theoretical eclecticism is important to encouraging thriving student affairs practice. Therefore, we are not limiting the monograph to the work of positive psychology or appreciative inquiry, but including other complementary approaches to understanding human and organizational behavior.

Each chapter is designed to introduce central positive psychological constructs, discuss relevant empirical research, and translate key concepts into concrete recommendations for practice. Although the scope of this monograph does not allow for capturing the entire breadth of this evolving discipline, we hope that the following chapters will inspire the reader to explore a new theoretical paradigm that can contribute to flourishing professional practice.

The first chapter of the monograph, authored by Jennifer Bloom, Bryant Hutson, Ye He, and Erin Konkle, presents a framework for organizing positive psychology and appreciative inquiry-inspired educational practice: appreciative education. Bloom and colleagues provide introductory and foundational ideas from positive psychology and appreciative inquiry that are presented with more specific applications in later chapters.

Chapters Two and Three focus on applications of appreciate inquiry (AI) and positive psychology for the development of positive higher education institutions. In Chapter Two, Matthew Fifolt and Lori Lander discuss applications of AI for organizational improvement. They use two case studies to illustrate the antecedents, dynamics, and results of AI interventions. In Chapter Three, Peter Mather and Michael Hess describe a common problem on college campuses, binge drinking, and discuss how positive psychology–inspired leadership practices can result in fresh approaches to dealing with organizational challenges.

Chapters Four and Five delve into recent scholarship on the positive traits of students that result in engaged learning, academic success, and degree completion. In Chapter Four, Laurie Schreiner discusses how to boost the experience of thriving among college students. Curiosity and thriving are two important correlates of student learning, and thus connect positive psychology to this fundamental goal of higher education practice. Chapter Five introduces a nuanced understanding of the character strength of curiosity found in high-achieving college students. Eileen Hulme, Daniel Green, and Kimberly Ladd provide practical suggestions for nurturing this strength for educational success.

Chapters Six and Seven deal with pedagogies growing out of positive psychology and appreciative inquiry scholarship. In Chapter Six, Laura

Harrison and Shah Hasan address the use of appreciative approaches in classroom teaching. In Chapter Seven, Peter Mather and Erin Konkle discuss ways in which appreciative understandings of education and community development can inspire new and effective community service practices.

A wealth of positive psychology literature has been published over the last 15 years. In Chapter Eight, we present a variety of resources that can be useful to educators wanting to explore the discipline beyond the contents of this sourcebook. The chapter includes seminal works from positive psychology, appreciative inquiry, and asset-based community, as well as both philosophical and practical resources to aid educators in their journeys to promote thriving students and enriching learning communities.

We hope that higher education faculty and administrators who read this monograph will find inspiration for new approaches to professional practice. We look forward to hearing your stories about how practicing education from an appreciative approach has worked for you.

Peter C. Mather
Eileen Hulme
Editors

References

Cooperrider, D. L., Whitney, D., and Stavros, J. M. *Appreciative Inquiry Handbook.* Bedford Heights, Ohio: Lakeshore Publishers, 2003.

Keyes, C.L.M., and Haidt, J. *Flourishing: Positive Psychology and the Life Well-Lived.* Washington, D.C.: American Psychological Association, 2002.

Ryff, C. D., and Singer, B. "Ironies of the Human Condition: Well-Being and Health on the Way to Mortality." In L. G. Aspinwall and U.M. Staudinger (eds.), *A Psychology of Human Strengths: Perspectives on an Emerging Field* (pp. 271–288). Washington, D.C.: American Psychological Association, 2002.

Seligman, M.E.P. *Authentic Happiness: Using the New Positive Psychology to Realize Your Potential for Lasting Fulfillment.* New York: Simon & Schuster, 2002.

Seligman, M.E.P. *Flourish: A Visionary New Understanding of Happiness and Well-Being.* New York: Free Press, 2011.

PETER C. MATHER *is an associate professor of Higher Education and Student Affairs and secretary to the board of trustees at Ohio University.*

EILEEN HULME *is the executive director of the Noel Academy for Strengths-Based Leadership and Education and a professor in the Department of Doctoral Higher Education at Azusa Pacific University.*

1

Appreciative education is presented as a framework for leading higher education institutions, delivering truly student-centered services, and guiding higher education professionals' interactions with students.

Appreciative Education

Jennifer L. Bloom, Bryant L. Hutson, Ye He, Erin Konkle

Higher education professionals play a pivotal role in efforts to retain students, but should retention be the primary focus? After all, the definition of the word *retain* (Dictionary.com, 2012) is: "to keep possession of ... to continue to hold or have ... to hold in place or position." Such deficit-based thinking has led to the massive growth of programming for students that emphasizes topics such as "surviving" college, "recovering" from probation, or academic "remediation."

Rather than holding students in place, higher education is positioned to help students become their best selves and achieve their dreams, goals, and potentials. This growth requires a culture where employees and institutions are unified in their approach to empowering students. It also requires identifying and capitalizing on the strengths of students and higher education professionals to foster the development of the best qualities of individuals and the organization.

Indeed, education should be a learning experience through which students, faculty, and staff learn together and support and challenge each other. This chapter will highlight appreciative education (AE), an organizational and individual framework for creating a culture with high standards that simultaneously embraces ongoing learning, change, and improvement. The purpose of this chapter is to describe AE, including its theoretical infrastructure, as well as provide strategies for implementing it to guide innovative individual and organizational practices.

What Is Appreciative Education?

Appreciative education is a framework for delivering high-quality education on both an individual and organizational level. It provides an intentional and positive approach to bettering educational enterprises by

NEW DIRECTIONS FOR STUDENT SERVICES, no. 143, Fall 2013 © Wiley Periodicals, Inc.
Published online in Wiley Online Library (wileyonlinelibrary.com) • DOI: 10.1002/ss.20055

focusing on the strengths and potential of individuals and organizations to accomplish co-created goals. This interactive and transformative process functions by permeating educational organizations. In this section, we provide an overview of the theoretical grounding of AE as a theory, practice, and mindset, as well as highlight the six phases of AE.

Theoretical Grounding and Appreciative Mindset. The AE framework has deep theoretical roots, including social constructivism, positive psychology, and appreciative inquiry. *Social constructivism* is the foundational theoretical perspective that guides AE and echoes Dewey's (1916, p. 46) observation that "education is not an affair of 'telling' and being told, but an active and constructive process." In other words, AE is built on the notion that knowledge is constructed through collaboration. By creating an interactive teaching and learning process both inside and outside the classroom, learners can actively link new ideas and concepts that they encounter to existing ones, forming connections between the past, present, and future. Appreciative education builds on the affirmative aspects of prior understanding to trigger positive connections between new concepts and past experiences, and to project positive images of future potential development as a source of motivation for learning new material.

While social constructivism guides our understanding of the nature of the learning process, positive psychology and appreciative inquiry have led us to challenge the deficit-based, problem-solving-oriented mentality at both individual and organizational levels. Discontent with the psychology profession's concentration on "repairing damage within a disease model of human functioning" (Seligman and Csikszentmihalyi, 2000, p. 5), Seligman and Csikszentmihalyi proposed the notion of positive psychology as a way "to begin to catalyze a change in the focus of psychology from preoccupation only with repairing the worst things in life to also building positive qualities" (p. 5).

Focusing on individuals' "authentic happiness," Seligman (2002) detailed three measurable elements of happiness, including positive emotion, engagement, and meaning. *Positive emotion* entails how we feel; *engagement* describes the "flow" we experience when we are able to leverage our top strengths to the degree that we overlook the passage of time when focused on an activity; and *meaning* refers to individuals' desire to pursue a greater purpose in life. All three elements compose life satisfaction and can be measured using various self-report inventories (http://www. authentichappiness.sas.upenn.edu/Default.aspx).

Building on his own theory, Seligman (2011) more recently argued that it is *well-being*, rather than happiness, that should be the primary focus of positive psychology. The well-being theory involves five pillars: *positive emotion, engagement, positive relationships, meaning and purpose,* and *accomplishment*. Instead of viewing happiness as a singular dimension focusing on individuals' self-perception, the well-being theory posits that socially constructed and shared norms, values, and beliefs are also important. The ultimate goal for individuals, therefore, is no longer maximizing happiness. Rather, it is to flourish through the development of the five pillars in one's well-being, including both self-perception and social recognition.

Seligman and his colleagues (2009) have been leaders in applying positive psychology in educational settings, and have coined the term *positive education* as a means to help students develop skills that will increase their sense of well-being. His research team designed and implemented the Penn Resiliency Program and Positive Psychology Program in experimental control studies, finding that the Penn Resiliency Program reduced symptoms of depression, hopelessness, and anxiety (Brunwasser and Gillham, 2008), and the Positive Psychology Program enhanced students' engagement in learning and improved their social skills (Seligman and others, 2009).

Proving that well-being programs can be taught and their impact can be measured, Seligman and his team have continued their research to identify measurable growth in students' well-being and their engagement in learning. While their research at the Geelong Grammar School in Australia—where positive education is implemented at the school level—has demonstrated the potential of applying positive psychology for school change, positive education research in general tends to focus more on individual development rather than organizational change (Kristjansson, 2012; Mather, 2010; Oades, Robinson, Green, and Spence, 2011). AE provides a framework for delivering on the principles of positive education on both the individual and organizational levels.

Different from the focus on individual well-being emphasized through positive education, *appreciative inquiry* was developed by Cooperrider and Srivastva (1987) as an organizational development theory that "provides a positive rather than a problem-based lens on the organization, focusing members' attention on what is possible rather than what is wrong" (van Buskirk, 2002, p. 67). Viewing educational settings as living organizations, appreciative inquiry has been applied widely in education to guide pedagogy (Conklin, 2009; Neville, 2008), collaborations (Calabrese, 2006; Calabrese and others, 2008), professional development (Giles and Kung, 2010), student affairs (Elleven, 2007), and action research methods (Giles and Alderson, 2008; San Martin and Calabrese, 2011).

Building on Cooperrider and Srivasta's (1987) work, Bloom, Hutson, and He (2008) adapted appreciative inquiry from an organizational development model to a model for guiding individual interactions with college students called appreciative advising. Appreciative advising gives academic advisors and other student affairs professionals a set of concrete tools and strategies for developing positive relationships with students.

A key component undergirding both appreciative inquiry and appreciative advising is the appreciative mindset. The appreciative mindset plays heavily into creating positive interactions with others. It posits that if people are looking for the worst in others, they will find the worst. Many of us have been conditioned to identify quickly the faults in others; the appreciative mindset reminds us to instead actively seek out the best in other people.

AE is a powerful synthesis of the social constructivist, positive psychology, appreciative inquiry, and appreciative advising approaches. AE provides both a theoretical infrastructure and a flexible framework for educational practice. Instead of focusing on either individual or organizational development, AE celebrates the development of a framework that is interactive, transformational, adaptable, and can be used to guide both individual interactions and organizational efforts.

The Six Phases of Appreciative Education. Guiding both individual and organizational practices, AE also follows some practical guidelines. Built on the 6-D model of appreciative advising, which has its origins in the 4-D model of appreciative inquiry, the six phases of AE are: *Disarm, Discover, Dream, Design, Deliver*, and *Don't Settle*. These phases do not represent a step-by-step methodology, but rather serve as general principles that guide the AE approach.

The Disarm phase recognizes that power differentials do exist on both individual and organizational levels, so this phase emphasizes reminding participants to be especially cognizant of the importance of creating safe environments where all members feel that their voice is valued and respected. On both individual and organizational levels, power differentials do exist, so the Disarm phase reminds participants to be especially cognizant of the importance of creating safe environments where all members feel that their voice will be heard. Engaging and coaching others about the importance of using positive verbal and nonverbal immediacy behaviors, especially early in interactions where people tend to be the most suspicious of each other, can establish a respectful culture to maximize teaching and learning relationships.

The Discover phase emphasizes the importance of using positive, open-ended questions focused on learning other people's perceptions of their own personal strengths and the strengths of the organization of which they are a member. This enhances the development of interdependence within people and their organization. Internally, individuals can identify personal strengths and assets at cognitive, metacognitive, and affective levels through self-reflective instruments or strengths-based self-reflection questions.

On the institutional level, it is important for individuals to situate themselves within the best of the larger organizational context and identify why they are proud of their connection to the organization. One could argue that some individual strengths are context specific and may be uncovered only through social interactions with others in the larger organizational context. In educational settings, the Discover component is especially important to keep in mind as we model and encourage the recognition of both individual and organizational strengths.

The Dream phase highlights the importance of uncovering personal and organizational visions. While goals tend to be more concrete and objective, dreams can include visions that are much bigger, and sometimes may even be perceived as nebulous or unrealistic. We each have unique visions for our lives and the organizations where we work. Working together in differing roles and settings within our institutions, it is important that we draw from similarities across our dreams and create shared visions for the organization that can guide positive changes.

The Design phase is typically described as an action plan where individual strengths are aligned to achieve both individual and shared dreams; the process is socially constructed and self-evolving. The designed plan may provide concrete guidance for the daily actions we take, but more important, it serves as a means for us to further uncover our strengths and dreams, rather than serve as a means to an end.

The Deliver phase entails thoughtful actions taken not only to carry out the individual and organizational plans created during the Design phase; it emphasizes the importance of personal and organizational resilience as obstacles and challenges arise. Positively constructed social interactions encourage and motivate us to redefine roadblocks as signals for activating alternative thinking and reconceiving challenges as opportunities.

The heart of the Don't Settle phase is "positive restlessness" (Kuh and others, 2005) within and among individuals and organizations. Discovery of the past and dreaming of the future are impacted by one's perception of the present. As individuals and organizations grow, they are challenged to revisit the process of Disarm, Discover, Dream, Design, and Deliver so that they may revisit their assumptions, rediscover strengths and passions, create bigger dreams and shared visions, chart future steps, and keep seeking creative ways to accomplish goals.

Appreciative Education: Ideas for Innovative Practices

One of the most exciting aspects of AE is that it provides a flexible framework for delivering innovative practices that develop individuals and organizations and optimize performance. Six innovative practice ideas relevant to higher education are covered in this section: positive interactions, reciprocal learning, holistic engagement, strategic design, appreciative leadership, and intentional change. Note that the application of the AE framework is not limited to these six innovative practice ideas; we hope that they will be a launching point for readers to reflect on how the model can be used in other creative ways.

Positive Interactions. Innovative practices at both the individual and organizational levels begin with, and are completely dependent on, people's establishing positive communication patterns with each other (Kratzer, Leenders, and van Engelen, 2004). Thus, the first innovative practice is rightly titled positive interactions. Specific ways in which positive interactions at the individual level can be implemented in higher education institutions include utilizing an appreciative performance evaluation process, offering tools and time for self-reflection and self-assessment, and creating common spaces that encourage individuals to interact and collaborate.

At the organizational level, positive interactions foster a culture that is built on respect and appreciation for every member of the team (Cameron, Dutton, and Quinn, 2003). Conflict occurs within any group, but in appreciative organizations it is openly and honestly discussed with the focus on moving through the conflict and into resolution. Meeting agendas reflect the needs of all team members and are built around the mission, vision, and values of the unit to ensure focus and efficiency.

Perhaps not surprisingly, positive interactions have been found to help students, staff, and institutions thrive. In the *Appreciative Advising Revolution* Bloom, Hutson, and He, 2008, explored and evaluated the centrality of positive interactions to promoting student academic achievement and organizational development. Similarly, Saunders and Hutson (2012) found that these positive interactions between professional advisors and at-risk students were germane to helping students enhance relationships with faculty, staff, and peers and ultimately improve their academic standing.

Meetings, especially those with potentially contentious issues on the agenda, should start with the facilitator's reminding attendees: "Let's all proceed with the presumption of goodwill" (Autry, 1991, p. 157). Autry (1991) points out that if we assume that people come to the table with goodness in their hearts, intentionally establishing a positive tone for the meeting will lift the level of dialogue, even if there are difficult issues that need to be addressed. Another organizational strategy involves creating an appreciative employee recognition program where all members of the community are responsible for recognizing the good efforts of their co-workers both publicly and personally.

Reciprocal Learning. At their best, teaching *and* learning is a shared responsibility between the instructor and the student. This necessitates embedding reflective questions within conversations between professionals and students. Appreciative college instruction used the six-phase framework format of appreciative advising as a model for taking a positive approach to teaching college-level student success courses (Bloom, Hutson, He, and Robinson, 2011). We posit that the positive, open-ended questions that are the infrastructure for appreciative advising and appreciative college instruction represent a powerful tool for engaging parties in both teaching and learning (Bloom, Hutson, and He, 2008; Bloom, Hutson, He, and Robinson, 2011). This is largely due to the fact that these open-ended questions invite others to share their stories, which have been the most frequently used form of communication for human beings since the dawn of time: "There have been great societies that did not use the wheel, but there have been no societies that did not tell stories" (LeGuin, n.d., para.

6). Thus, stories are an important part of our fiber as human beings and they help us learn about ourselves and others.

On an individual level, those that teach and mentor students inside and outside the classroom need to view these duties as opportunities to learn and grow. This can be accomplished by regularly reflecting on what we are learning from our students and by asking questions that will elicit their stories. Critical reflection empowers higher education professionals to not only commit to a life of continuous learning themselves, but also to cultivate the reflective habits of college students (Hutson, Bloom, and He, 2009). These reflective opportunities can be provided through the discussion of current news, blogs, and trends that influence higher education (D. Pruitt, personal communication, July 1, 2012); the reflection on personal practical theories that guide our interactions and practices; and in community-engaged action research projects that utilize strength-based inquiry methods (He, 2013). Not only is committing to staying current imperative to do our jobs well, we also must realize that we are powerful role models for our students.

The key to thriving organizations is a commitment to provide multiple opportunities for all members of the group to teach and learn. Tichy (2002, p. 3) proposes the concept of the teaching organization rather than the learning organization. To be an effective teacher, one needs to be a world-class learner, but that is not sufficient. One also has to share what is being learned and inspire others to be teachers, too.

Departments within the institution can embody this commitment to continuous learning by setting up a book club with a rotating facilitator; actively encouraging employees to present their work, not only at conferences, but to each other, and/or write about their successes for publications; or visiting other offices that are potential collaborators. Another technique involves taking time to identify each team member's unique strengths and talents, and then sharing this information with others so that team members can call on each other to share their knowledge and expertise.

Holistic Engagement. Holistic engagement involves helping professionals and students make the most of their experiences. For students, this involves encouraging them to connect and integrate their in- and out-of-class experiences with their values and their career and life goals. Likewise, for professionals, the emphasis is on helping them connect their on- and off-the-job experiences with their values and goals.

On an individual level, we know that higher education professionals who adopt the appreciative mindset and engage in appreciative practices reported that they were able to better utilize their strengths and talents and formed more positive relationships with co-workers, families, friends, and others (Howell, 2010). Mimicking Google's policy that allows employees to spend 20 percent of their working hours on their own innovative ideas and projects (Berkun, 2008), higher education institutions can encourage staff to spend one to four hour(s) per week pursuing new ideas or volunteering in their community. This will not only increase individual productivity, it can also serve as a way to increase organizational productivity.

Students can serve as peer engagement coaches for their colleagues, giving them the opportunity to share their expertise and knowledge of campus resources with fellow students. Staff and students can put together their own e-portfolios that document their learning, achievements, and progress toward meeting personal and professional goals. Another option is to have students fill out a student engagement plan (O'Keefe, 2009) that helps them identify possible involvement opportunities that are congruent with their strengths, passions, and interests. Service learning opportunities are a meaningful way to bring together faculty, staff, and students to meet the needs of community-based organizations as well as to give opportunities for all parties to build connections with each other (Bringle and Hatcher, 2000).

At the organizational level, institutions can offer shadowing opportunities for staff interested in learning about unfamiliar areas. Divisions may also implement a process wherein staff members are encouraged to write a portion of their own job description to include projects and programs that they find most stimulating and beneficial. Further, traditional committees can be replaced with dynamic work groups that focus on output and outcomes. These work groups can promote an appreciative culture by keeping meetings to a minimum and ensuring that those that are held are focused on a clear agenda that includes input from all team members. Appreciative education practices can also be applied to training orientation leaders (Propst Cuevas and others, 2011) and engaging families and communities (Buyarski, Bloom, Murray, and Hutson, 2011).

Strategic Design. In *Alice's Adventures in Wonderland*, Lewis Carroll wrote, "If you don't know where you're going, any road will get you there." Intentionality is woven throughout AE, but is especially important in strategic design. Drawing from the field of Human Resource Development, we define strategic design as intentionally created, future-driven plans to achieve goals and maximize organizational potential through individual development (Peterson, 2008). After all, an organization is merely a collective of the individuals that comprise it. Strategic design plans must be aligned to the organization's mission, vision, and values, and be student centered. Although the literature describes positive approaches to strategic planning initiatives in higher education settings (Atkins, 2010; Ellis, 2010), we are using the term *strategic design* because a plan indicates a specific path to be followed, while design suggests a specific purpose to be achieved—in this case, optimal student development.

Strategic design should be inclusive and allow for all team members to participate in strategy development and execution, from the president to the support staff. Individuals that interact with students on a daily basis are often more in tune with their needs and areas of oversight than a management team. In terms of strategy and motivation, it makes the most sense to have individual team members play a key role in establishing goals, setting a path to achieve them, and executing the plan. As Bandura (1997) says, "When people select their own goals, they are likely to have greater self-involvement in achieving them. If goals are prescribed by others, however, individuals do not necessarily accept them or feel obligated to meet them" (p. 28).

Individuals should bear great responsibility in the strategic design of their specific area, but it would be shortsighted to stop there. Allowing team members to offer input in the creation of the larger organizational design can foster congruence, engagement, and a shared vision. In practice, these unit designs and overarching organizational designs should dovetail one another. Using a collective approach to the design process will also encourage cooperation and reduce replication. This can be achieved by hosting a large brainstorming session or online discussion board.

Organizations can adopt strategic design initiatives including a SOAR (strengths, opportunities, aspirations, and results) analysis in lieu of the traditional SWOT (strengths, weaknesses, opportunities, and threats) analysis (Stavros and Hinrichs, 2009). Planning an appreciative inquiry summit is another way for an organization to collectively engage in the strategic design process (Ludema, Whitney, Mohr, and Griffin, 2003). Strategic designs should be flexible enough to allow for innovation, yet structured enough to avoid chaos. Designs should include assessment tools and appropriate budgetary support. Evaluation is a critical component of strategic design in AE. The integration of ongoing appreciative assessment and evaluation not only captures the success of programs and units, but also offers immediate feedback for program improvement and development (Hutson and He, 2011; Saunders and Hutson, 2012).

Appreciative Leadership. Leadership, whether at the individual or organizational level, is most powerful when we recognize our connectedness to others. Thus, we view all leadership as collective. According to the Kellogg Foundation (2007), "collective leadership becomes possible when the members of a group, motivated by a common purpose, begin to build relationships with each other that are genuinely respectful enough to allow them to co-construct their shared purpose and work" (p. 3). Each member brings a unique set of ideas and experiences to the group, and thus it takes a village to make higher education institutions run smoothly.

Appreciative leadership promotes a student-centered approach to educational leadership. There is one question that should be used to make decisions: "Is this in the best interest of the students we serve?" If the answer is no, that is a clear indicator that the right answer has not yet emerged. Appreciative leadership offers a philosophy that is both intentional and inclusive (Schiller, Holland, and Riley, 2002; Whitney, Trosten-Bloom, and Rader, 2010). All perspectives are valued and considered when choosing the path forward, whether for an individual or an organization. Recognizing that every person is able to create and transfer knowledge generates an environment of equity and encourages organizational citizenship (Podsakoff, MacKenzie, Paine, and Bachrach, 2000).

At the individual level, appreciative leadership can be fostered by spending the necessary time and resources to develop individual employees. Institutions can encourage mentoring relationships that provide professional staff members with a role model and sounding board. Institutions can also offer trainings—including professional and personal development exercises—to facilitate individual growth. Individuals who are developing in this way and are confident in themselves and their abilities are best positioned to actively participate in the organization and contribute to the whole. In *Good to Great*, Jim Collins (2001) identifies the need to not only have the right people on the team, but to have them in the right places where they are able to use their strengths. Organizations that foster individual leadership development are able to be more effective in implementing a collective leadership model.

There are many ways for organizations to transition to a collective, appreciative leadership style. One easy way to begin the transition is to rotate the leader of each staff meeting, allowing all team members the opportunity to serve in an important leadership role, including collecting agenda items, printing the agenda, and running the meeting. Another strategy is to allow staff members to lead projects outside of their specific job tasks that are of particular interest to them and report back to the entire staff. Promoting collaborations across units and even institutions would further strengthen the collective leadership in enhancing appreciative education in all higher education settings. The implementation of appreciative advising in multiple institutions (Bloom and others, 2009) and the collaborative development of the Appreciative Advising Inventory across campuses (He, Hutson, and Bloom, 2010) are good examples of how institutions could work together in promoting positive change utilizing collective resources.

Intentional Change. AE is steeped in theories of constant and intentional positive organizational change (Whitney and Trosten-Bloom, 2010). Once educational institutions have adopted an AE approach, a virtuous cycle of change can develop where each success builds on other successes, and failures provide excellent opportunities to learn and propel new change (Cameron, Bright, and Caza, 2004).

To encourage employees to come up with innovative ideas for change and improvement, time should be provided for them to dream about an idealized future on both a personal and an organizational level. Organized dreaming retreats allow individuals to reinvent themselves and to see new opportunities in their work, keeping them fresh and energized. During a retreat, previous successes should be celebrated and used to identify and launch new ideas and goals.

NEW DIRECTIONS FOR STUDENT SERVICES • DOI: 10.1002/ss

On an individual level, employees can be primed to be more accepting of change through educational initiatives about the phases of change and the emotions that accompany them. Change is typically not easy for people, but by teaching individuals the emotions involved in the stages of change and offering breakthrough strategies, organizations can help employees deal with personal and organizational transitions.

Conclusion

Appreciative education presents a powerful new framework for enhancing individual and organizational effectiveness. Steeped in the theories of social constructivism, positive psychology, appreciative inquiry, and appreciative advising, this approach can be used to lead administrative and academic units as well as enhance interactions of institutional members with students and other constituents. However, it is the theory-to-practice nature of the framework that facilitates its implementation to optimize the effectiveness of the organization as well as the individuals that comprise the organization. Fueled by a shared commitment to student success and approaching obstacles as opportunities for growth, AE is destined to transform the ways in which higher education will be delivered in the future.

References

Atkins, K. *Strategically Planning to Change.* New Directions for Student Services, no. 132, 17–25. San Francisco: Jossey-Bass, 2010. doi: 10.1002/ss372

Autry, J. A. *Love and Profit: The Art of Caring Leadership.* New York: Avon Books, 1991.

Bandura, A. *Self Efficacy: The Exercise of Control.* New York: Worth, 1997.

Berkun, S. *Thoughts on Google's 20% time.* Retrieved from http://scottberkun.com/2008/thoughts-on-googles-20-time/, March 12, 2008.

Bloom, J. L., Hutson, B. L., and He, Y. *The Appreciative Advising Revolution.* Urbana-Champaign, Ill.: Stipes, 2008.

Bloom, J. L., and others. "How Eight Institutions Have Incorporated Appreciative Advising." *The Mentor: An Academic Advising Journal,* 2009, *11*(2).

Bloom, J. L., Hutson, B. L., He, Y., and Robinson, C. W. *Appreciative College Instruction: Becoming a Force for Positive Change in the Classroom.* Urbana-Champaign, Ill.: Stipes Publishing, 2011.

Bringle, R. G., and Hatcher, J. A. "Institutionalization of Service Learning in Higher Education." *Journal of Higher Education,* 2000, *71*, 273–290.

Brunwasser, S. M., and Gillham, J. E. "A Meta-analytic Review of the Penn Resiliency Program." Paper presented at the Society for Prevention Research, San Francisco, Calif., 2008.

Buyarski, C. A., Bloom, J. L., Murray, J. E., and Hutson, B. L. "Engaging Families in Supporting Their Students: An Appreciative Approach" (Invited Article). *Journal of College Orientation and Transition,* 2011, *19*(1), 75–85.

Calabrese, R. L. "Building Social Capital Through the Use of an Appreciative Inquiry Theoretical Perspective in a School and University Partnership." *International Journal of Educational Management,* 2006, *20*(3), 173–182. doi: 10.1108/09513540610654146

Calabrese, R. L., and others. "Emerging Technologies in Global Communication: Using Appreciative Inquiry to Improve the Preparation of School Administrators." *Inter-*

national Journal of Educational Management, 2008, 22(7), 696–709. doi: 10.1108/09513540810908593

Cameron, K. S., Bright, D., and Caza, A. "Exploring the Relationships Between Organizational Virtuousness and Performance." *American Behavioral Scientist,* 2004, 47, 766–790.

Cameron, K. S., Dutton, J. E., and Quinn, R. E. (eds.). *Positive Organizational Scholarship.* San Francisco: Berrett-Koehler, 2003.

Collins, J. *Good to Great: Why Some Companies Make the Leap and Others Don't.* New York: HarperCollins, 2001.

Conklin, T. A. "Creating Classrooms of Preference: An Exercise in Appreciative Inquiry." *Journal of Management Education,* 33(6), 772–792, 2009. doi: 10.1177/1052562909333888

Cooperrider, D. L., and Srivastva, S. "Appreciative Inquiry in Organizational Life." In Woodman, R. W., and Pasmore, W. A. (eds.), *Research in Organizational Change and Development* (pp. 129–170). Greenwich, Conn.: JAI Press, 1987.

Dewey, J. *Democracy and Education: An Introduction to the Philosophy of Education.* New York: Free Press, 1916.

Dictionary.com. "Retain." 2012. Retrieved from http://dictionary.reference.com/browse/retaining?s=t

Elleven, R. K. "Appreciative Inquiry: A Model for Organizational Development and Performance Improvement in Student Affairs." *Education,* 2007, 127(4), 451–455.

Ellis, S. E. *Introduction to Strategic Planning in Student Affairs: A Model for Process and Elements of a Plan.* New Directions for Student Services, no. 132, 5–16. San Francisco: Jossey-Bass, 2010. doi: 10.1002/ss.371

Giles, D., and Alderson, S. "An Appreciative Inquiry into the Transformative Learning Experiences of Students in a Family Literacy Project." *Australian Journal of Adult Learning,* 2008, 48(3), 465–478.

Giles, D., and Kung, S. "Using Appreciative Inquiry to Explore the Professional Practice of a Lecturer in Higher Education: Moving Towards Life-centric Practice." *Australian Journal of Adult Learning,* 2010, 50(2), 308–321.

He, Y. "Developing Teachers' Cultural Competence: Application of Appreciative Inquiry in ESL Teacher Education." *Teacher Development,* 2013, 17(1), 55–71.

He, Y., Hutson, B. L., and Bloom, J. L. "Appreciative Team Building in Learning Organizations." In P. Hagen and T. Kuhn (eds.), *Scholarly Inquiry in Academic Advising: NACADA Monograph Series M20* (pp. 133–141). Manhattan, Kans.: National Academic Advising Association, 2010.

Howell, N. "Appreciative Advising from the Academic Advisor's Viewpoint: A Qualitative Study" (Unpublished doctoral dissertation). University of Nebraska, Lincoln, 2010.

Hutson, B. L., and He, Y. "Appreciative Advising Inventory: Identifying College Student Assets for Successful Transition." *Journal of College Orientation and Transition,* 2011, 19(1), 23–36.

Hutson, B. L., Bloom, J. L., and He, Y. "Reflection in Advising." *Academic Advising Today,* 2009, 32(4), 12.

Kellogg Leadership for Community Change. (2007). The Collective Leadership Framework: A Workbook for Cultivating and Sustaining Community Change. Battle Creek, Michigan: W.K. Kellogg Foundation. Retrieved from: http://www.wkkf.org/knowledge-center/resources/2007/04/the-collective-leadership-framework-a-workbook-for-cultivating-and-sustaining-community-change.aspx

Kratzer, J., Leenders, R.T.A.J., and van Engelen, J.M.L. "Stimulating the Potential: Creative Performance and Communication in Innovation Teams." *Creativity and Innovation Management,* 2004, 13, 63–71.

Kristjansson, K. "Positive Psychology and Positive Education: Old Wine in New Bottles?" *Educational Psychologist,* 2012, 47(2), 86–105. doi: 10.1080/00461520.2011.610678

Kuh, G. D., and others. *Student Success in College: Creating Conditions That Matter.* San Francisco: Jossey-Bass and American Association for Higher Education, 2005.

LeGuin, U. K. "Patti's Favorite Storytelling Quotes." n.d. Retrieved from http://www.pattistory.com/54-Quotes.htm

Ludema, J. D., Whitney, D., Mohr, B. J., and Griffin, T. J. *The Appreciative Inquiry Summit: A Practitioner's Guide for Leading Large-Group Change.* San Francisco: Berrett-Koehler, 2003.

Mather, P. C. "Positive Psychology and Student Affairs Practice: A Framework of Possibility." *Journal of Student Affairs Research and Practice,* 2010, 47(2), 157–173. doi: 10.2202/1949–6605.6019

Neville, M. G. "Using Appreciative Inquiry and Dialogical Learning to Explore Dominant Paradigms." *Journal of Management Education,* 2008, 32(1), 100–119.

Oades, L. G., Robinson, P., Green, S., and Spence, G. B.*Towards a Positive University. Journal of Positive Psychology: Dedicated to Furthering Research and Promotion Good Practice,* 2011, 6(6), 432–439. doi: 10.1080/17439760.2011.634828

O'Keefe, S. "Creating a Tool to Help Your Advisees Become Engaged on Your Campus." *The Mentor,* 2009. Retrieved from http://dus.psu.edu/mentor/old/articles/090107so.htm

Peterson, S.L. "Creating and Sustaining a Strategic Partnership: A Model for Human Resource Development." *Journal of Leadership Studies,* 2008, 2, 83–97.

Podsakoff, P. M., MacKenzie, S. B., Paine, J. B., and Bachrach, D. G. "Organizational Citizenship Behavior: A Critical Review of the Theoretical and Empirical Literature and Suggestions for Future Research." *Journal of Management,* 2000, 26, 513–563.

Propst Cuevas, A. E., and others. "Adapting and Implementing Appreciative Advising Framework to Train Orientation Leaders." *Journal of College Orientation and Transition,* 2011, 19(1), 86–98.

San Martin, T. L., and Calabrese, R. L. "Empowering At-Risk Students Through Appreciative Inquiry." *International Journal of Educational Management,* 2011, 25(2), 110–123. doi: 10.1108/09513541111107542

Saunders, D., and Hutson, B. L. "Uncovering Assets of College Students Through Learning Contracts: An Application of Appreciative Advising." *Journal of Appreciative Education,* 2012, 1(1), 1–13.

Schiller, M., Holland, B. M., and Riley, D. *Appreciative Leaders: In the Eye of the Beholder.* Taos, N.M.: Taos Institute, 2001.

Seligman, M.E.P. *Authentic Happiness: Using the New Positive Psychology to Realize Your Potential for Lasting Fulfillment.* New York: Free Press, 2002.

Seligman, M.E.P. *Flourish: A Visionary New Understanding of Happiness and Well-Being.* New York: Free Press, 2011.

Seligman, M.E.P., and Csikszentmihalyi, M. "Positive Psychology: An Introduction." *American Psychologist,* 2000, 55, 5–14.

Seligman, M.E.P., Ernst, R.M., Gillham, J., Reivich, K., and Linkins, M. "Positive Education: Positive Psychology and Classroom Interventions." *Oxford Review of Education,* 2009, 35, 293–311.

Stavros, J. M., and Hinrichs, G. *The Thin Book of SOAR: Building Strengths-Based Strategy.* Bend, Oreg.: Thin Book, 2009.

Tichy, N. M. *The Leadership Engine.* New York: HarperCollins Publishers Inc., 2002.

van Buskirk, W. "Appreciating Appreciative Inquiry in the Urban Catholic School." In R. Fry, F. Barrett, J. Seiling, and D. Whitney (eds.), *Appreciative Inquiry and Organizational Transformation: Reports from the Field* (pp. 67–97). Westport, Conn.: Quorum Books, 2002.

Whitney, D., and Trosten-Bloom, A. *The Power of Appreciative Inquiry: A Practical Guide to Positive Change.* San Francisco, CA: Berrett-Koehler, 2010.

Whitney, D., Trosten-Bloom, A., and Rader, K. *Appreciative Leadership: Focus on What Works to Drive Winning Performance and Build a Thriving Organization*. New York: McGraw-Hill, 2010.

JENNIFER L. BLOOM *is clinical professor and director of the Higher Education and Student Affairs Program at the University of South Carolina.*

BRYANT L. HUTSON *is director of research at Credo.*

YE HE *is assistant professor in the Department of Teacher Education and Higher Education at the University of North Carolina at Greensboro.*

ERIN KONKLE *is a doctoral candidate in Organizational Leadership, Policy, and Development at the University of Minnesota.*

2

The purpose of this chapter is to describe the utility and scope of appreciative inquiry (AI) and outline the benefits of this strengths-based approach to engage in meaningful self-assessment.

Cultivating Change Using Appreciative Inquiry

Matthew Fifolt, Lori Lander

Institutions of higher education have increasingly experienced calls for greater accountability, transparency, and data-informed decisions (Schroeder, 2010). Faced with similar levels of scrutiny, student affairs divisions are equally compelled to examine the efficiency and effectiveness of their operations and to adapt their approaches in order to ensure that programs and services are consistent with and supportive of institutional priorities (Green, Jones, and Aloi, 2008; McLaughlin, McLaughlin, and Kennedy-Phillips, 2005; Pike and others, 2011; Sandeen, 2004).

One tool available for conducting a thorough and honest self-evaluation is appreciative inquiry (AI), a strengths-based approach to organizational planning and assessment. AI provides student affairs professionals with the requisite skills and resources to build on institutional assets and to strive toward becoming high-performing organizations in which partnerships, cross-functional collaborations, and responsive units are the rule rather than the exception (Whitt, 2006).

In this chapter, we describe the elements of AI as an organizational self-assessment technique and then illustrate how student affairs professionals from two separate universities used AI as a tool for assessment and organizational improvement. Through these two case studies, we demonstrate how the articulation and increased awareness of collective organizational values, facilitated through the AI process, led to increased support for organizational and institutional priorities at both institutions.

Appreciative Inquiry

AI is a coordinated approach to organizational change that utilizes reflection, introspection, and collaboration to leverage collective strengths. As

New Directions for Student Services, no. 143, Fall 2013 © Wiley Periodicals, Inc.
Published online in Wiley Online Library (wileyonlinelibrary.com) • DOI: 10.1002/ss.20056

such, it provides a methodology that is theoretically sound, field tested, and flexible enough to accommodate organizations of all types and sizes. Watkins and Mohr (2001) describe AI as a life-centric approach to organizational change in which systems harness positive emotions to increase coherence and energy.

AI is often visualized through a 4-D model; the four phases that comprise the model include Discovery, Dream, Design, and Destiny (Cooperrider and Whitney, 2005). Each phase of the 4-D model addresses a specific task. In the Discovery phase, individuals share stories and illustrations of personal experiences to examine *the best of what is*. In the Dream phase, individuals consider the ideal vision for their organization and articulate *what could be*. In the Design phase, individuals develop an organizational framework that can harness the strengths of its *positive core*; the Design phase communicates *what should be*. Finally, in the Destiny phase, individuals implement the vision as a way to move the organization toward positive change; the Destiny phase represents *what will be* (Cooperrider and Whitney, 2005).

As a tool for organizational assessment, AI is a philosophy that describes *why* change happens and a process that underscores *how* change happens. Martinez (2002) notes:

> AI is a change process. It is not another organizational development intervention: rather it is a new approach to existing organizational development interventions such as strategic planning, business process redesign, teambuilding, organizational restructuring, individual and project evaluation (valuation), coaching, diversity work, and so on. (p. 35)

Key Principles of AI

Watkins, Mohr, and Kelly (2011) identify the six key principles of AI as: (1) constructionist, (2) simultaneity, (3) poetic, (4) anticipatory, (5) positive, and (6) wholeness. These principles are described in greater detail below, and the properties of each principle are highlighted in the case studies that follow.

Constructionist. The constructionist principle purports that individuals create meaning through their interactions with one another and that the world is shaped and defined by social discourse. In AI, individuals are both participants in and recipients of this socially constructed reality. The stories individuals tell "lead to agreement about how we [individuals] will see the world, how we will behave, what we will accept as reality and what we will believe to be possible" (Bugge, Canine, and Sloan, 1994, para 1.)

Simultaneity. The principle of simultaneity suggests that the process of inquiry, in and of itself, creates change. If reality is socially constructed in the context of relationships and communication (Cooperrider, Barrett, and Srivastva, 1995), then the questions individuals ask become inputs into the process of inquiry. Further, the nature and tone of the questions (either positive or negative) directly influences the direction toward which individuals expend their energy.

Poetic. In AI, storytelling serves as the means by which individuals gather holistic information from one another, including not only facts but also "feelings and affect that a person experiences and the recognition that stories (like all good poetry) can be told and interpreted about any aspect of an organization's existence" (Watkins, Mohr, and Kelly, 2011, p. 74). By sharing stories and experiences with one another, AI encourages individuals to look at their organization and its people *at their best* and focus on what they want more of (Kelm, 2005). Through creativity and innovation, the poetic principle allows an organization to interpret and reinterpret itself (Krattenmaker, 2001).

Anticipatory. The anticipatory principle states that people and organizations tend to move in the direction of their positive images of the future. In other words, individuals will work toward what they see and believe they can do (Orem, Binkert, and Clancy, 2007). Kotter and Cohen (2002) call this "painting pictures of the future" (p. 67). According to Watkins and colleagues (2011), "The most important resources we have for generating constructive organizational change or improvement are our collective imagination and our discourse about the future" (p. 73).

Positive. Simply put, the positive principle describes a process in which individuals choose to envision possibilities for a positive future rather than dwell on the negative aspects of their current situation. AI empowers individuals to innovate about what *should be*, rather than focus on what *is not*. McAllister (2011) notes that this positive mindset can influence all aspects of an organization, including performance, persistence, learning, and resilience to setbacks.

Wholeness. AI recognizes an organization as a whole system in which individuals can come together to identify a positive, central core and common vision for the organization's future. The premise of wholeness is that what may appear to be a *part* is really "some small piece of a larger whole and that it is our choice about whether to see the part or to embrace the whole" (Watkins, Mohr, and Kelly, 2011, p. 75). Whitney and Trosten-Bloom (2003) suggest that wholeness evokes trust because it ensures that all individuals share responsibility for both the process and the resulting product.

Planning and Organization

Conventional strategic planning models emphasize overcoming one's weaknesses in order to achieve organizational success. By contrast, AI is a strengths-based planning model that suggests just the opposite: focusing on the positive and building on strengths (Fifolt and Stowe, 2011). Grandy and Holton (2010) describe this approach as challenging "the traditional deficit perspective in organizational and change management" (p. 180).

AI as a Framework. In addition to using AI as a stand-alone process for organizational reform, multiple authors have highlighted the use of AI as a framework for applying additional techniques and methods for group planning. For example, in *Appreciative Inquiry in Higher Education*, Cockell and MacArthur-Blair (2012) illustrate how the 4-D model of AI can be used to scaffold the SOAR model for organizational planning.

SOAR. SOAR (strengths, opportunities, aspirations, and results) is a strategic planning framework for eliciting thoughtful responses from stakeholders regarding the most positive and valuable aspects of their organization. In practice, SOAR could be used to evoke conversations among stakeholders about what they want to discover or learn about within their organization, their desired future for the organization, and how they want to see the organization grow and flourish. These conversations are critical in developing affirmative topics that ultimately set the agenda for "learning, knowledge sharing, and action" (Cooperrider and Whitney, 2005, p. 17). Whitney and Trosten-Bloom (2003) combine SOAR with the 4-D model of AI and envision these parallel processes as follows:

Strengths (Discovery)—the best of what is
Opportunities (Dream)—what could be
Aspirations (Design)—what should be
Results (Destiny)—what will be

The current authors suggest that SOAR operationalizes the six key principles of AI by providing a structure and a process for individuals to engage in meaningful dialogue about positive change. The well-defined parameters of SOAR can lessen anxiety inherent in all change initiatives by first explaining the methods and then engaging individuals in the actual process of change. As demonstrated in the case studies, removing the barriers of fear and uncertainty allows individuals to establish trust and thereby share value-rich stories that stretch the organization beyond the status quo.

AI Resources

AI relies explicitly on input from individuals at all levels to uncover the organization's *positive core* (strengths). Through *appreciative interviews*, stakeholders share experiences and stories in order to develop a new and compelling vision for the organization's future (Cooperrider and Whitney, 2005). AI encourages individuals to ask the question: "How can we be at our best all of the time?"

As Bolman and Deal (2001) state, "In successful organizations, people's sense of significance is rooted in shared stories, passed from person to person and generation to generation" (p. 119). While "[t]here is no right way to move from collecting the stories, themes, dreams, and hopes of [individuals within] the institution to producing a written final plan" (Cockell and McArthur-Blair, 2012, p. 149), the burgeoning AI community has created numerous tools and resources to organize the AI process. The current authors provide examples of resources at the end of this chapter, including: (a) interview protocol, (b) interview summary sheet, and (c) checklist for interviewers (see Resources).

Organizing Data. AI requires a great deal of organization and planning in order to conduct rigorous data collection and for data analysis to occur; therefore, the authors recommend that organizations create a central repository for information. Systematic methods for data storage will streamline data collection processes and ensure that information sharing is consistent and straightforward among stakeholders. Making information accessible throughout the organization can strengthen personal connections between staff members and result in greater collaboration and teamwork. Importantly, once an organization has established a plan and identified ways to collect and manage data, it must determine how the socio system components (such as roles, responsibilities, management systems and policies, etc.) and technical system components (such as business processes and technology) can be used to execute the plan (Martinez, 2002).

In Short

AI is a strengths-based approach to organizational development that replaces the traditional top-down model of power and control with one that gives all participants an equal stake, and therefore an equal voice, in the process. AI is designed for systematic change but the outcomes, and even the methods, are not predetermined; it requires individuals to invest time and effort into discovering what gives life to their organization when it is most effective (Cooperrider and Srivastva, 1987). AI maintains a systems orientation that focuses on changing the organization rather than changing the people (Martinez, 2002). In short, AI engages and empowers individuals to imagine possibilities rather than dwell on problems (Watkins and Mohr, 2001). The following section presents examples of how student affairs professionals at two separate universities used AI to facilitate self-assessment initiatives within their organizations.

Examples of AI in Student Affairs

University of Oregon. In 2010, the director of Residence Life at the University of Oregon (UO) utilized appreciative inquiry to support and enhance student learning related to the on-campus living experience. Changes in key leadership positions throughout university housing created an opportunity for developing a coherent philosophical vision that intentionally created and supported student learning. The overall goal was to develop a residence life program that threaded learning throughout every aspect of the organization, from hiring and training of student staff to collaboration among the residence life leadership team and faculty members interested in developing residential learning communities.

The director of Residence Life introduced the principles of AI to the professional residence life staff during two half-day retreats. Staff members were asked to respond to a series of intentionally designed open-ended prompts, including:

1. Think of a time when you were truly engaged and alive in your job and with your organization (Discovery).
2. Imagine the organization as you most want it to be (Dream).
3. Structure the organization to maximize our dreams of enhancing student learning (Design).
4. Detail how the organization supports and actualizes student learning (Destiny) (Cooperrider, Whitney, and Stavros, 2003).

By sharing stories about the numerous ways in which student learning occurs in the residence halls (including co-curricular activities linked to course syllabi, academic residential programs, learning communities, and small-group conversations sponsored by faculty), the Residence Life staff developed a greater understanding of its collective values in support of the academic mission of the university. Professional staff recognized that they could be true contributors to student learning alongside faculty colleagues. Since students spend the majority of their time outside of the classroom, members of the Residence Life staff agreed that they had an excellent opportunity to enhance student learning in the residential setting.

The director of Residence Life continued to facilitate this dialogue, and the Residence Life leadership team soon realized that most students are thirsty for knowledge and engagement. By hearing each other's stories and dreaming of what *could be*, the leadership team began to align Residence Life programs, services, and activities with the academic mission of the university. The Residence Life program shifted its emphasis from being "student centered" to being an organization that was centered on student learning.

As a result of these learning-focused conversations, the Residence Life leadership team developed a set of shared learning outcomes to articulate the skills, knowledge, and behavior it wanted students to learn while living in the residence halls. Learning outcomes resulting from these conversations included self-knowledge; interpersonal connections with one another; and thoughts, decisions, and actions that intentionally align with behaviors, values, and aspirations. Additionally, the AI process allowed the team to address difficult, and at times uncomfortable, decisions about Residence Life operations and programs. However, by using learning outcomes to guide decisions, the team has collectively phased out or replaced programs, services, and activities that do not contribute to the ultimate goal of student learning.

Equipped with the language of learning outcomes, the culture of the residence life program has changed, especially with regard to students' perceptions and goals for learning. The inclusive nature of AI has allowed the Residence Life staff to identify all stakeholders (residents, parents, alumni, student staff, professional staff, administrators, and faculty) and engage them in meaningful conversations (constructivist). This process of change has also positively influenced the ways in which stakeholders communicate with and relate to one another (positive, simultaneity).

As the Residence Life program continues to evolve to better meet the needs of student residents, team members are collaborating with faculty and staff in the Dean of Student's office in new and unprecedented ways. For example, Residence Life staff members are working with various educational partners on campus to identify collaborative learning opportunities for students to enhance their academic experience while living on campus.

Interpersonal and cultural exchanges among professional and student staff in Residence Life have also improved. As a staff of mostly live-in professionals, staff members now see Residence Life from a whole systems perspective and consider the welfare of the organization rather than focusing solely on individual units. Specifically, supervision and professional development is now managed by a team of assistant directors, and decisions that affect the larger organization are made by representative committees. Additionally, all residence life policies have been updated to reflect students' needs related to learning within a residential community. With AI as the compass, the UO Residence Life staff is cultivating student learning by collaborating with faculty and role-modeling positive behaviors for students. The Residence Life leadership team believes that anything is possible, and its benchmarks for student learning have become measureable signs of success.

University of Alabama at Birmingham (UAB). Similar to UO, student affairs professionals at the University of Alabama at Birmingham (UAB) used AI to develop a shared vision and values statement, not with a single unit or department, but with the entire division of student affairs. In response to a request by the vice president for student affairs to better "tell our story," an internal leadership group called the Vision Team and 30 staff facilitators conducted *appreciative interviews* with each member of the division of student affairs. Facilitators also led focus groups, structured interviews, and strategic polling of external stakeholders to collect data from more than 500 participants over the course of eight weeks.

Consistent with the principles of AI, the Vision Team worked diligently to gather input from individuals at all levels of the organization—from senior-level administrators to front-line staff—and across stakeholder groups to ensure that everyone had a voice in the process and a vested interest in the outcome (constructionist) (Fifolt, 2011). By examining the student affairs division from multiple perspectives and through multiple observers (Patton, 1990), the Vision Team was able to view the organization from various points of view (simultaneity).

Through *appreciative interviews,* facilitators encouraged individuals to share personal stories that were reflective of the organization's *positive core.* These personal stories often illustrated situations in which student affairs professionals provided information or assistance to a student that ultimately influenced the student's decision or ability to persist. With few exceptions, these personal stories were rich in detail and provided key insights into staff members' interactions with others within the organization (positive, poetic, wholeness).

Members of the Vision Team developed multiple channels of communication so that individuals could ask questions and share information as well as clarify thoughts and challenge assumptions. Team members sent multiple drafts of the shared vision and values statements to all stakeholders, posted the statements to a dedicated website, and discussed the proposed statements during town hall–type meetings with stakeholder groups. These multiple forums created a continuous feedback loop for the AI process and ensured that individuals had multiple opportunities to react and respond to the relevance of themes incorporated in the vision and values statement drafts (anticipatory).

AI provided the student affairs division with an approach to organizational review that was systematic and authentic. By discussing core strengths and by searching for ways to maximize those strengths, members of the student affairs division were moving in the direction of organizational authorship (Fifolt and Stowe, 2011). The vision and values statement articulated the division's organizational values and expressed members' perceptions of what the organization was and what they hoped it would become (Mintzberg, 1994). Further, members of the division could recount these compelling statements of strategic intent because everyone had played a critical role in creating them.

Conclusion

Based on these experiences at UO and UAB, the authors believe that AI is consistent with the rich, descriptive nature of student affairs work. Personal stories revitalized organizational cultures at both institutions by tapping into the abundant pool of knowledge and experiences that existed among organizational members. Through the AI process, individuals were able to share keen insights and observations, many of which had never been considered before, to articulate organizational values. These values, in turn, enabled student affairs members to define and build on organizational strengths and align programs, services, and activities with core institutional priorities.

References

Bolman, L. G., and Deal, T. E. *Leading with Soul: An Uncommon Journey of Spirit*. San Francisco: Jossey-Bass, 2001.

Bugge, I., Canine, T., and Sloan, B. "Principles of Appreciative Inquiry in Coaching." Symposium conducted at the 2nd International Conference on Appreciative Inquiry, Miami, FL, September 1994.

Cockell, J., and McArthur-Blair, J. *Appreciative Inquiry in Higher Education*. San Francisco: Jossey-Bass, 2012.

Cooperrider, D. L., Barrett, F., and Srivastva, S. "Social Construction and Appreciative Inquiry: A Journey in Organizational Theory." In D. Hosking, P. Dachler, and K. Gergen (eds.), *Management and Organization: Relational Alternatives to Individualism*. Aldershot, England: Avebury, 1995.

Cooperrider, D. L., and Srivastava, S. "Appreciative Inquiry in Organizational Life." *Research in Organizational Change and Development*, 1987, *1*, 129–169.

Cooperrider, D. L., and Whitney, D. *Appreciative Inquiry: A Positive Revolution in Change*. San Francisco: Berrett-Koehler, 2005.

Cooperrider, D. L., Whitney, D., & Stavros, J. M. *Appreciative Inquiry Handbook*. Bedford Heights, Ohio: Lakeshore, 2003.

Fifolt, M. "Re-invigorate Your Strategic Planning Process: Appreciative Inquiry Promotes Collaboration." *Leadership Exchange: Solutions for Student Affairs Management*, 2011, *9*(1), 40.

Fifolt, M., and Stowe, A. M. "Playing to Your Strengths: Appreciative Inquiry in the Visioning Process." *College & University*, 2011, *87*(1), 37–40.

Grandy, G., and Holton, J. "Mobilizing Change in a Business School Using Appreciative Inquiry." *Learning Organization*, 2010, *17*(2), 178–194.

Green, A. S., Jones, E., and Aloi, S. "An Exploration of High-Quality Student Affairs Learning Outcomes Assessment Practices." *NASPA Journal*, 2008, *45*(1), 133–157.

Kelm, J. *Appreciative Living: The Principles of Appreciative Inquiry in Personal Life*. Wake Forest, NC: Venet, 2005.

Kotter, J. P., and Cohen, D. S. *The Heart of Change: Real-Life Stories of How People Change Their Organizations*. Boston: Harvard Business School Publishing, 2002.

Krattenmaker, T. "Change Through Appreciative Inquiry." *Harvard Management Communication Letter*, 2001, *4*(10), 5–6.

McAllister, K. "Appreciative Inquiry Principles: 5. The Positive Principle, 2011." Retrieved from www.positive-engagement.com/

McLaughlin, G., McLaughlin, J., and Kennedy-Phillips, L. "Developing Institutional Indicators: The Role of Institutional Research." Paper presented at the Annual Forum of the Association for Institutional Research, San Diego, Calif., May/June 2005.

Martinez, C. F. "Appreciative Inquiry as an Organizational Development Tool." *Performance Improvement*, 2002, *41*(8), 34–39.

Mintzberg, H. *The Rise and Fall of Strategic Planning*. New York: Free Press, 1994.

Orem, S. L., Binkert, J., and Clancy, A. L. *Appreciative Coaching: A Positive Process for Change*. San Francisco: Jossey-Bass, 2007.

Patton, M. Q. *Qualitative Evaluation and Research Methods* (2nd ed.). Newbury Park, Calif.: Sage, 1990.

Pike, G. R., Kuh, G. D., McCormick, A. C., Ethington, C. A., and Smart, J. C. "If and When Money Matters: The Relationships Among Educational Expenditures, Student Engagement and Students' Learning Outcomes." *Research in Higher Education*, 2011, *52*(1), 81–106.

Sandeen, A. "Educating the Whole Student: The Growing Academic Importance of Student Affairs." *Change*, 2004, *36*(3), 28.

Schroeder, C. C. "Bridging the Assessment Gap: The Key to Organizational Learning and Performance Improvement." Paper presented at the meeting of the ACPA Assessment Institute, Charlotte, NC, June 2010.

Watkins, J., and Mohr, B. *Appreciative Inquiry: Change at the Speed of Imagination*. San Francisco: Jossey-Bass, 2001.

Watkins, J., Mohr, B., and Kelly, R. *Appreciative Inquiry: Change at the Speed of Imagination* (2nd ed.). San Francisco: Jossey-Bass, 2011.

Whitney, D., and Trosten-Bloom, A. *The Power of Appreciative Inquiry: A Practical Guide to Positive Change*. San Francisco: Berrett-Koehler, 2003.

Whitt, E. "Are All of Your Educators Educating?" *About Campus*, 2006, *10*(6), 2–9.

MATTHEW FIFOLT *is associate director of the Evaluation and Assessment Unit in the Center for the Study of Community Health at the University of Alabama at Birmingham.*

LORI LANDER *is director of Residence Life and Academic Initiatives at the University of Oregon. Lori is pursuing her PhD at Colorado State University.*

RESOURCES

Sample Interview Protocol

Thank you for meeting with me and participating in this process of gathering information from colleagues across the Division. These interviews are part of an intense effort to discover our internal best practices in order to:

- Articulate a compelling vision and mission for the Division
- Clearly define the contributions of Student Affairs
- Unify our branding among the departments within the Division
- Better share our story across the university

To start, I'd like to learn about your beginnings in the Division of Student Affairs. When did you come to work for the Division and what attracted you to Student Affairs? What keeps you in the Division?

- What made it an exciting experience?
- What was it about YOU that made it a peak experience?
- What were the most important factors in the organization that helped make it a peak experience?

Sample Affirmative Topic Questions (Discovery)

1. Meaningful Relationships
Think of a time when you took part in fostering a mutually beneficial relationship, a time in your life (at work or in your personal or community life) when you not only met the other person(s) halfway, but also met and exceeded needs on both sides. Describe the situation in detail. Who was involved? How did you interact differently? What were the outcomes and benefits you experienced?

2. Customer Service
Think of a time when you experienced truly excellent customer service, a time in your life (at work or in your personal or community life) when the service exceeded your expectations. Describe the situation in detail. Who was involved? How did you interact differently? What were the outcomes and benefits you experienced?

Future (Dream)
As we move into the future, what is one wish you have for the best future of Student Affairs? What does the ideal future of Student Affairs look like to you? Be descriptive.

Materials adapted from *Telling the Student Affairs Story: Celebrating our Past...Envisioning our Future*. Vision Planning in the Division of Student Affairs at UAB, 2009. Developed by Dr. Angela M. Stowe and Vision Team.

Sample Interview Summary Sheet

Complete and submit to:
Name of Interviewer (your name): _____
Date of Interview: _____
Interviewee's Department/Unit: _____

What was the most quotable quote that came out of this interview?

What was the most compelling story that came out of this interview? (Use as much space as you need.)

Overall, what was the sense of what was most important to this individual?

What three positive themes stood out most for you during the interview related to each of the following?

Meaningful relationships

    1. _____

    2. _____

    3. _____

Customer service

    1. _____

    2. _____

    3. _____

Vision of the Future

    1. _____

    2. _____

    3. _____

Materials adapted from *Telling the Student Affairs Story: Celebrating our Past…Envisioning our Future*. Vision Planning in the Division of Student Affairs at UAB, 2009. Developed by Dr. Angela M. Stowe and Vision Team.

3

Drawing from positive organizational scholarship, the authors describe strategies for moving from an ineffective focus on problems to leveraging organizational strengths for productive change.

Promoting Positive Leadership

Peter C. Mather, Michael Hess

It is a fundamental premise of positive psychology that a negative bias exists among individuals and organizations (Seligman, 2002, 2011). People have a tendency to emphasize the negative over the positive and to evaluate themselves and others according to their deficiencies rather than their strengths. As a corollary, organizations often prefer to hold onto the safety of the status quo in lieu of venturing into what could be, because they tend to give considerable power to potential negative outcomes (Linley, Harrington, and Garcea, 2010). These tendencies and the consequences of the negativity bias are often not recognized or understood by those who hold them. As a result, constraints are placed on the ability of organizations to flourish. We illustrate these pitfalls and strategies for avoiding them through a case study of Janice, a vice president for student affairs.

Janice's Concern

Janice is the vice president for student affairs at a major, comprehensive university that recently received notoriety as the number-one party school by a national periodical. Upon hearing this inauspicious announcement, Janice flashed back five years to the first time that the institution was placed on the "party school" list. Following the initial publication, much attention was given to finding ways to remove the institution from the list. For instance, financial resources were provided to the student health and wellness program in order to offer more face-to-face education to students exhibiting high-risk drinking behaviors. In addition, the university instituted an aggressive conduct policy, which included contacting students' parents, levying monetary fines, and implementing a quick-trigger suspension (i.e., two alcohol-related violations equals suspension from the institution). Also, addiction specialists were hired in the counseling center to

New Directions for Student Services, no. 143, Fall 2013 © Wiley Periodicals, Inc.
Published online in Wiley Online Library (wileyonlinelibrary.com) • DOI: 10.1002/ss.20057

address some of the underlying mental health issues that often manifest with unhealthy drinking patterns.

But now, a few years after the implementation of this programmatic effort, Janice is left with more questions than answers. Although there is evidence of modest improvement in the alcohol culture (e.g., reports of alcohol violations in the residence halls have decreased), the university continues to see pervasive problems associated with high-risk drinking among its student population, and the "party school" reputation has been difficult to dispel. Of course, this university is not alone. Alcohol abuse has been a major concern within higher education in the United States for decades (Wechsler and others, 2002). Despite significant efforts brought to bear on the issue, improvements have been marginal (Wechsler and others, 2002), and institutions often look to divisions of student affairs to lead efforts to ameliorate the problem. This leaves not only Janice, but a host of other student affairs leaders from around the country to try to find new ways of addressing an age-old problem.

Positive Organizational Scholarship

It is in this context that we explore positive organizational scholarship (POS) as a guide for framing the work of leaders in higher education and student affairs in dealing with issues such as the one facing Janice and her colleagues. POS is one of the three pillars of the subdiscipline of positive psychology. Whereas much of positive psychology focuses on individual human strengths and well-being, POS applies the same principles to organizational functioning. As has been the case with psychology's historic deficiency orientation, Cameron, Dutton, and Quinn (2003) noted that far less attention has been given to the goal of organizational thriving than to remediating organizational problems. While both dimensions of institutional study are important, attention to the incidence of organizational strengths is crucial for the future of organizational leadership practice. We draw from the body of POS to present possible ways of dealing with the daunting problem that Janice and her colleagues face.

Leadership Models

Consider the cultures of which Janice is a part. She is a member of an institution that is deeply concerned about the potentially harmful activities of many of its students. In addition, she is part of a professional field—student affairs—which is charged with ensuring high-quality experiences for students, but is also in the position of having to defend its role and function in the context of an institution that is under close watch by suspicious stakeholders.

Today's higher education environment presents many threats and challenges. According to Block (2008), however, immersing oneself in fixing problems is in itself problematic. Block maintained:

> The core belief from which we operate is that an alternative or better future can be accomplished by more problem-solving [. . .] This context—that life is a set of problems to be solved—may actually limit any chance of the future being different from the past. The interest we have in problems is so intense that at some point we take our identity from those problems. (p. 33)

Bateman and Porath (2003) echo Block's sentiment, differentiating between a *prevention* focus—which deals with safety, responsibilities, and obligations—and a *promotion* focus that attends to accomplishments and aspirations. POS does not recommend ignoring the problems. For example, Lewis (2011) encourages a balanced perspective, but points out that positive approaches are often deemphasized and underused. Lewis notes that positivity is not about ignoring problems and pretending they do not exist. Rather, it is about achieving a functional ratio of positive to negative emotions. The ability to find and model a balanced perspective in the face of difficulties is a hallmark of positive organizational leadership.

Because of the negativity bias that is inherent in individuals and organizations, intentional efforts are required in order to make a meaningful change in institutional practice. Although we believe that leadership can be leveraged from any place in the organization, it is optimal for the formal leader—in this case, Janice—to be at the forefront of her organization's change.

The POS concept of authentic leadership provides a model for considering one's role as a leader in a languishing organization that identifies heavily with its problems. Leadership is not simply about solving problems, but about recognizing and leveraging organizational assets (McKnight and Block, 2011). For instance, it would be common for Janice to address the problem of her campus's drinking culture by simply investing more of her own time and energy, as well as her employees' talents, in focusing on a solution. Alternatively, authentic leadership principles would suggest that it is time for Janice to step back from the problem and examine its context and even her own role in it. Authentic leaders are:

> Individuals who are deeply aware of how they think and behave and are perceived by others as being aware of their own and others' values/moral perspective, knowledge, and strengths; aware of the context in which they operate; and who are confident, hopeful, optimistic, resilient, and high on moral character. (Avolio and others, 2004, p. 802)

This notion of leadership highlights the importance of self awareness and a purposeful values center—something that can be easily lost when one's work is solely centered on solving problems. Boyatzis and McKee (2005) described the phenomenon of losing oneself in work as "dissonant leadership," where one's core values become undermined by a problem-centered focus. They contend:

> The most successful among us are often the ones who most easily lose our-
> selves along the way. Usually as a result of good intentions and doing what
> we are supposed to do—building a great career, committing to an organiza-
> tion [. . .] we can easily create fairly narrow, one-sided lives. Slowly, over the
> years, we can lose touch with who we are at our core and what we really care
> about, and one day find that we are not ourselves anymore. (p. 58)

When our protagonist, Janice, recognizes that she is overly identifying with the problem of her campus's alcohol culture, she also recognizes that this has taken a toll on her professional and personal life. While she has achieved personal success (she acquired her leadership position at a fairly young age), she realizes that her drive to work in student affairs was cen-tered on something greater than the problems to which she has invested so much of her time and energy.

In order to move out of dissonance and into authentic leadership, or what Boyatzis and McKee (2005) call "resonant leadership," Janice must seek a way to connect to her core values, which will provide energy and renewal in her own work so that she can translate this into her work with others. In many cases, student affairs professionals are drawn to the field out of compassion and hope (Taub and McEwen, 2006), so we will assert that these are core values for Janice. Compassion is a value at the root of one's entry into a helping profession. We believe that hope is central because student affairs is part of an educational enterprise that is centered on a belief that people can learn and grow into a better future.

According to Snyder (1994), hope is made up of two components: willpower and pathways. The willpower component corresponds to the desire to accomplish a certain outcome and to one's belief that it is achiev-able. The pathways component refers to an individual's ability to find alter-native paths to reach the goal. So Janice can help to foster hope within her division by enacting it through her sincere declarations of vision and pur-pose that exceed defining the organization as something "not to be"—such as a party school. Lewis (2011) points out that engaging one's community in the co-creation of organizational ideals is essential. She states, "If we can't imagine our positive workplace, positive culture or positive future, we certainly can't create it" (p. 211). In thinking about the problem in this new way, Janice is taking an important first step toward creating a better organi-zation and grounding her leadership in authenticity.

Janice's decision to adopt authentic and resonant leadership principles may be met with resistance, so the "pathway" dimension of hope will also be tested. From her superiors (i.e., the university president and trustees) to colleagues and staff within her division, many might consider the change in Janice's approach to be unsettling. It may indeed run counter to the dominant narrative of problem solving in the institution. In this con-text, POS also uses the term *courageous principled leadership* (Bateman and Porath, 2003) as a framework for thinking about the phenomenon Janice is

NEW DIRECTIONS FOR STUDENT SERVICES • DOI: 10.1002/ss

experiencing and the actions she should adopt. In the context of a culture that reveres "doing something, anything," Janice cannot be paralyzed by her newfound suspicion of singular focused problem solving or by resistance from others. Rather, Janice must be determined to stay connected to core, underlying values as she leads the division through this process. Rather than just framing the work as "reducing problem drinking," Janice will ensure that it is defined differently. She will envision her role as *providing life-enhancing opportunities for emerging adults.*

Abundance and the Upward Spiral

Janice is determined to move away from a problem-centered approach and focus on possibilities and aspirations that may reenergize her own life and work. She also she cannot be the sole source of leadership in this new way of thinking, but must engage the values and energy of institutional colleagues, divisional staff, and students in the process. Therefore, in addition to working on her own mindset and approach, she turns her attention to others who will be important allies in her task.

The idea that leadership is a collective enterprise is an essential dimension of the appreciative orientation. POS not only believes in the potential for authenticity and strengths in the leader, but also relies on the strengths of members of the community. Linley, Harrington, and Garcea (2010) highlight two fundamentally different orientations: one centered on deficits and the other on abundance. The deficit approach is captured in Janice's initial interventions in which she attempted to overcome the challenges through conventional problem-solving approaches. Conversely, the abundance approach reflects the orientation of appreciative inquiry: "identifying peak experiences . . ., and creat[ing] an ideal, desired future characterized by extraordinary performance" (Linley, Harrington, and Garcea, 2010, p. 4).

Higgs (2010) noted that nearly three-quarters of change initiatives fail. Appreciative inquiry, as discussed by Fifolt and Lander in Chapter 6 of this volume, is recommended as one important approach to ensuring successful cultural change. POS also highlights the value of building positive emotional life within the organization as a means for fostering success (Fredrickson, 2003; Sekerka and Fredrickson, 2010).

One of the important findings from POS is that an organization that is defined by positive affect is not only a pleasant work environment; it also is a foundation for creativity and productivity. According to the Broaden and Build Theory (Sekerka and Fredrickson, 2010), positive emotions broaden one's intellectual and problem-solving repertoire. Sekerka and Fredrickson noted that "the power to create deep and sustainable change resides in the emotional dimension of the workplace enterprise" (p. 85). This suggests that the road to enhancing effectiveness in creating a healthy and vibrant university community can be approached, at least in part, through building a positive work environment.

NEW DIRECTIONS FOR STUDENT SERVICES • DOI: 10.1002/ss

Lewis (2011) illustrated a variety of approaches to boosting organizational positivity. These approaches focus on two related principles: (1) maximizing community members' strengths and (2) creating a strong social fabric. When practiced in organizations, these two principles help form the foundation of a work environment that centers on an organizational culture that supports and encourages positive relationships.

Strengths. Organizations that focus on employee strengths by giving feedback centered on positive attributes rather than deficiencies produce several important outcomes (Hodges & Asplund, 2010), including lower turnover rates and higher productivity. One approach to promoting a strength-based organization is an adaptation of 360-degree feedback, a common performance appraisal model. In Linley's (2008) approach, individuals are not measured against targeted organizational competencies. Rather, they profit from portraits their colleagues create of their contributions to relationships and work. In this approach, individuals select several people, including peers, subordinates, and supervisors, who write responses in the form of short stories or vignettes to positively framed questions, such as:

- "When have you seen me making a special or important contribution, and what distinctive strengths did I display?"
- "When have you been most proud to know me, to call yourself my friend?"

By eliciting statements from friends and family, the individual may realize that strengths used in one context may be transferable to others. Lewis (2011) suggests that the resulting stories be analyzed by the individual who is being assessed. This allows the person to draw out his or her own strengths. Lewis notes that drawing out strengths in this way allows individuals to acknowledge their weaknesses as well. That is, when someone is bolstered by the awareness of their own strengths, they are not as likely to be threatened by acknowledging the areas that may need improvement.

Linley (2008) presents several other approaches to discovering the strengths people possess. One of these is the concept of *strength spotting* (p. 72). This practice includes "spotting strengths in people—whether oneself or others—as we go about our daily activities" (p. 74). Linley encourages the habit of actively engaging in strength spotting, noting that even when the strength is difficult to name, the art of seeing strengths in ourselves and others and "the impact of validation and recommendation that comes through having somebody identify a strength in you" (p. 77) has a powerful effect.

Approaches such as the 360-degree adaptation and other strengths analysis approaches rest on the belief that people should not necessarily be made to fit into positions, but that positions should be shaped by the gifts of the individuals who hold them. Lewis (2011) points out that while core

Figure 3.1. Strategies for Capitalizing on Organizational Strengths

- Conduct strengths assessments with members of organization, using tools such as Gallup's StrengthsFinder (Rath, 2007); Values in Action Inventory of Strengths (VIA Institute on Character), or Linley's Strengths Selector (Linley, 2008)

- Orient organizational members to practice Strengthspotting (Linley, 2008)

- Use an appreciative 360 degree performance appraisal tool (Linley, 2008)

- Practice role-shaping, by adapting job expectations to individual employees' strengths (Lewis, 2011; Linley, 2008)

skills may be required for a certain position, there can be different avenues to the accomplishment of tasks. This recognition can free leaders and workers to embrace flexibility in appreciating different pathways to success. A summary of recommendations for promoting a strengths-based organization is displayed in Figure 3.1.

Social Fabric. We contend that the building of a strong social fabric is critical if student affairs organizations hope to bring the full weight of their resources to bear on problems like those facing Janice. Dutton and Heaphy (2003) refer to high-quality connections (HQCs) as the foundation of positive organizations. They describe the primary features of HQC as (1) feelings of vitality and aliveness (i.e., positive energy), (2) sense of positive regard (i.e., feeling of being known or loved), and (3) experience of mutuality (i.e., full co-participation). When HQC is evident, participants demonstrate a higher immunity to environmental stressors and are more productive than when HQC is absent.

HQC is at the centerpiece of what Block (2005, 2008) calls a restorative community. While Block's work focuses specifically on community organizing rather than on organizational scholarship, the recommendations for building a restorative community can inform Janice's work with her division and institution. Block presents a dichotomy between what he calls the retributive community and the restorative community. A key difference between the two, according to Block, is that the retributive community is fragmented. In the words of Dutton and Heaphy (2003), it lacks high-quality connections. The undercurrent of fragmentation is evident in Block's (2005) analysis:

> The dominant existing public conversation is retributive, not restorative. It is void of accountability and soft on commitment. In this way it drives us apart, it does not bring us together. The existing conversation is about entitlement, not accountability. *To be accountable, among other things, means you act as an owner and part creator of whatever it is that you wish to improve.* (p. 3)

Block (2005, 2008) asserts that a rich social fabric requires a sense of ownership. This principle goes beyond the fundamentals of the strengths-based organization in which everyone finds a niche of value in their particular assets. Indeed, Block suggests that for organizations like Janice's to flourish, members of the community must be fully vested. So a primary task for leaders is to create engagement by sharing ownership or distributing leadership.

Social fabric and organizational engagement can be enriched through the implementation of particular appreciative models of practice. For example, strengths-based organizations highlight the assets of all members of the organization and thus send the message that their gifts are of value. Particular structural realities can also play a role in bolstering social fabric and engagement. Structural considerations include developing small, diverse, interdepartmental working teams that minimize the importance of status roles (Lewis, 2011; Senge, Flowers, Scharmer, and Jaworski, 2005); deemphasizing strict adherence to standard procedures (Baker, Cross, and Wooten, 2003; Block, 2008); enacting work-role fluidity (Lewis, 2011); and allocating inspiring team tasks (Block, 2008; Lewis, 2011).

While recognizing the importance of structural considerations for implementing productive changes, Block (2008) places an emphasis on how organizational life and work is narrated by community members. He recommends moving away from the following conventional approaches: telling the history of how we got here; giving explanations and opinions; blaming and complaining; making reports and descriptions; and carefully defining terms and conditions. These conventions help to ensure that productive and meaningful change will not occur.

In contrast, members of the organization should be focused on possibilities and be invited into deep and meaningful engagement with other community members in co-creating the new future. Specifically, one of Block's (2008) suggestions is that organizational members should be led into images of possibility rather than into solving problems. As an example, Janice and her colleagues have decided that rather than focusing on getting off of the party school list, they are going to put extensive energy into becoming a premier university involved in community service. This purpose was derived through a visioning process that included members of their division and valued colleagues across the institution. This hopeful aspiration grew out of their mutual awareness that their institution is situated in a high-poverty area and the acknowledgment that this effort might also be effective in ameliorating the drinking culture concerns, as well as providing an inspiring vision of positivity.

Other principles offered by Block (2008) are that dissent should be *encouraged* so that the agreed-upon alternatives have more power, and that members' gifts should be recognized and brought into the organization's work. The first of these principles can be realized only if members of the organization participate in the kind of personal work that Janice has assumed. That is, leaders in the student affairs division will be more apt to genuinely foster an environment of dissent if they are psychologically

Figure 3.2. Strengthening Social Fabric

- Allocate inspiring and meaningful work tasks (Baker, Cross, & Wooten, 2003)

- Recognize strengths and minimize status (Lewis, 2011)

- Foster creativity by de-emphasizing non-essential standard procedures (Lewis, 2011)

- Practice collective narratives associated with possibilities over problems (Block, 2008)

secure. Thus, there should be a team with the charge of envisioning and facilitating a divisional focus on well-being. These efforts can be guided by some of the rich sources emerging from positive psychology, such as Seligman's (2011) book, *Flourish,* or Achor's (2010) engaging and useful book, *The Happiness Advantage.* A list of recommendations for promoting social fabric is illustrated in Figure 3.2.

Conclusion

Positive organizational scholarship can be a powerful partner in catalyzing effective organizational change. Individuals often default to negative views of human nature, which result in ineffective and uninspired leadership practices. Due to our innate assumptions and resulting conventions of practice, it is important to approach leadership with intentional and sometimes counterintuitive approaches. We contend that leadership strategies that focus on fostering employee engagement and creativity will pay immense dividends for organizations. As stated by poet Nikki Giovanni (2007) after the tragedy at Virginia Tech in 2007, "We are better than we think and not quite what we want to be." POS rests on these fundamental ideas and presents new opportunities and challenges for Janice and her colleagues.

References

Achor, S. *The Happiness Advantage.* New York: Crown, 2010.

Avolio, B. J., Gardner, W. L., Walumbwa, F. O., Luthans, F., and May, D. R. "Unlocking the Mask: A Look at the Process by Which Authentic Leaders Impact Follower Attitudes and Behaviors." *Leadership Quarterly,* 15, 801–823, 2004.

Baker, W., Cross, R., and Wooten, M. "Positive Organizational Network Analysis and Energizing Relationships." In K. S. Cameron, J. E. Dutton, and R. E. Quinn (eds.), *Positive Organizational Scholarship: Foundations of a New Discipline* (pp. 328–342). San Francisco: Berrett-Koehler, 2003.

Bateman, T. S., and Porath, C. "Transcendent Behavior." In K. S. Cameron, J. E. Dutton, and R. E. Quinn (eds.), *Positive Organizational Scholarship: Foundations of a New Discipline* (pp. 122–137). San Francisco: Berrett-Koehler, 2003.

Block, P. "Civic Engagement and Restoration of the Community: Changing the Nature of the Conversation." 2005. Retrieved from http://www.peterblock.com/_assets/downloads/Civic.pdf

Block, P. *Community: The Structure of Belonging.* San Francisco: Berrett-Koehler, 2008.

Boyatzis, R., and McKee, A. *Resonant Leadership: Sustaining Yourself and Connecting with Others Through Mindfulness, Hope, and Compassion.* Boston: Harvard Business School Press, 2005.

Cameron, K. S., Dutton, J. E., and Quinn, R. E. "Foundations of Positive Organizational Scholarship." In K. S. Cameron, J. E. Dutton, and R. E. Quinn (eds.), *Positive Organizational Scholarship: Foundations of a New Discipline* (pp. 3–13). San Francisco: Berrett-Koehler, 2003.

Dutton, J. E., and Heaphy, E. D. "The Power of High-Quality Connections." In K. S. Cameron, J. E. Dutton, and R. E. Quinn (eds.), *Positive Organizational Scholarship: Foundations of a New Discipline* (pp. 263–278). San Francisco: Berrett-Koehler, 2003.

Fredrickson, B. "Positive Emotions and Upward Spirals in Organizations." In K. S. Cameron, J. E. Dutton, and R. E. Quinn (eds.), *Positive Organizational Scholarship: Foundations of a New Discipline* (pp. 263–278). San Francisco: Berrett-Koehler, 2003.

Giovanni, N. Convocation address, presented at Virginia Tech following the April 2007 tragedy. 2007. Available at http://www.remembrance.vt.edu/2007/archive/giovanni_transcript.html

Higgs, M. "Change and Its Leadership: The Role of Positive Emotions." In A. Linley, S. Harrington, and N. Garcea (Eds.), *Oxford Handbook of Positive Psychology and Work* (pp. 67–80). New York: Oxford University Press, 2010.

Hodges, T. D., and Asplund, J. "Strengths Development in the Workplace." In P. A. Linley, S. Harrington, and N. Garcea (eds.), *Oxford Handbook of Positive Psychology and Work* (pp. 3–9). New York: Oxford University Press, 2010.

Lewis, S. *Positive Psychology at Work: How Positive Leadership and Appreciative Inquiry Create Inspiring Organizations.* Chichester, England: Wiley-Blackwell, 2011.

Linley, P. A. *Average to A+: Realising Strengths in Yourself and Others.* Coventry, England: CAPP Press, 2008.

Linley, P. A., Harrington, S., and Garcea, N. "Finding the Positive in the World of Work." In P. A. Linley, S. Harrington, and N. Garcea (eds.), *Oxford Handbook of Positive Psychology and Work* (pp. 3–9). New York: Oxford University Press, 2010.

McKnight, J., and Block, P. *The Abundant Community: Awakening the Power of Families and Neighborhoods.* San Francisco: Berrett-Koehler, 2011.

Rath, T. *StrengthsFinder 2.0.* New York, Gallup Press, 2007.

Sekerka, L. E., and Fredrickson, B. L. Working positively toward workplace cooperation. In P. A. Linley, S. Harrington, and N. Garcea (eds.), *Oxford Handbook of Positive Psychology and Work* (pp. 81–94). New York: Oxford University Press, 2010.

Seligman, M.E.P. *Authentic Happiness: Using the New Positive Psychology to Realize Your Potential for Lasting Fulfillment.* New York: Free Press, 2002.

Seligman, M.E.P. Flourish: *A Visionary New Understanding of Happiness and Well-Being.* New York: Free Press, 2011.

Senge, P. M., Flowers, B., Scharmer, O., and Jaworski, J. *Presence: An Exploration of Profound Change in People, Organizations, and Society.* New York: Doubleday, 2005.

Snyder, C. R. *The Psychology of Hope.* New York: Simon and Schuster, 1994.

Taub, D., and McEwen, M. "Decision to Enter the Profession of Student Affairs." *Journal of College Student Development*, 2006, 47, 206–216.

VIA Institute on Character. http://www.viacharacter.org/www/

Wechsler, H., and others. "Trends in College Binge Drinking During a Period of Increased Prevention Efforts." *Journal of American College Health*, 2002, 50, 203–217.

PETER C. MATHER *is an associate professor of Higher Education and Student Affairs and secretary to the board of trustees at Ohio University.*

MICHAEL HESS *is an instructor in the Department of Educational Studies at Ohio University.*

NEW DIRECTIONS FOR STUDENT SERVICES • DOI: 10.1002/ss

4

This chapter describes the phenomenon of thriving as a deep engagement in learning experiences. The author also identifies multiple pathways to the acquisition of thriving and characteristics of communities that support thriving students.

Thriving in College

Laurie A. Schreiner

Grades and *grads*. These two words sum up the typical approach that most institutions of higher education have taken to define student success. Academic performance and graduation rates are easily measured and can be quantified for comparison purposes so that institutions—and entire nations—can gather a snapshot of their own "effectiveness." Yet most faculty and professional staff are keenly aware that this narrow focus misses an important element of the college student experience: whether students are vitally engaged in learning and making the most of their college education.

A more holistic view of student success is represented in the concept of *thriving* in college. Thriving is defined as being "fully engaged intellectually, socially, and emotionally in the college experience" (Schreiner, 2010a, p. 4). This view of student success looks beyond academic performance and graduation. Thriving students are engaged in the learning process, invest effort to reach important educational goals, manage their time and commitments effectively, connect in healthy ways to other people, are optimistic about their future and positive about their present choices, and are committed to making a meaningful difference in the world around them (Schreiner, 2010a).

Thriving as an Integrative View of Student Success

Representing an intersection of the principles of positive psychology and the goals of higher education, the concept of *thriving* was derived from research on *flourishing* (Keyes, 2003; Keyes and Haidt, 2003; Seligman, 2011) and the psychosocial factors most predictive of college student retention (Bean and Eaton, 2000; Berger and Milem, 1999). The goal of positive psychology is to enable a greater percentage of the world's population to

NEW DIRECTIONS FOR STUDENT SERVICES, no. 143, Fall 2013 © Wiley Periodicals, Inc.
Published online in Wiley Online Library (wileyonlinelibrary.com) • DOI: 10.1002/ss.20059

flourish (Seligman, 2011). Flourishing people have high levels of emotional, psychological, and social well-being. They are productively engaged with other people in their work and in society, experiencing fulfillment and a sense of purpose. They are also resilient, looking beyond themselves to help others find meaning, purpose, and satisfaction in life as well (Keyes, 2003). Seligman (2011) maintains that there are five elements of well-being that enable humans to flourish: positive emotion, engagement, meaning, accomplishment, and positive relationships. As applied to college students, I have chosen the word *thriving* for its shift in focus from merely surviving in college, and to distinguish it from the extensive research on flourishing in adult populations that does not include the academic and intellectual objectives inherent to the college experience. In measuring thriving across thousands of college students in hundreds of institutions in the United States, Canada, and Australia, this holistic definition of student success has been reliably assessed by the Thriving Quotient and its five scales of Engaged Learning, Academic Determination, Positive Perspective, Social Connectedness, and Diverse Citizenship (Schreiner, 2010a; illustrated in Figure 4.1). Each aspect is briefly described next.

Congruent with Seligman's (2011) *engagement* component in his well-being theory, *Engaged Learning* refers to "a positive energy invested in one's own learning, evidenced by meaningful processing, attention to what is happening in the moment, and involvement in learning activities" (Schreiner and Louis, 2011, p. 6). Students who are engaged in learning notice the environment around them; they pay attention to distinctions and are able to see multiple perspectives. They also process course content meaningfully, are energized by ideas, and draw connections between the content, their own lives, and other courses. This quality of learning is what Tagg (2003) refers to as *deep learning*, as it lasts beyond any one course and can transform a student's perspective on the world.

Academic Determination is similar to Seligman's (2011) *accomplishment* component of well-being, but it also includes an emphasis on goal setting, the ability to regulate one's own learning processes (Pintrich, 2004), investment of effort (Robbins and others, 2004), and time and

Figure 4.1. The Five Factors of Thriving

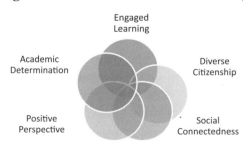

resource management (Ryff and Keyes, 1995). Students who are thriving academically have also learned how to apply their strengths to the academic tasks they face, which leads to higher levels of confidence and self-efficacy (Lopez and Louis, 2009).

Positive Perspective represents the ways in which thriving students view life. Congruent with Seligman's (2011) *positive emotion* component of well-being, students who are thriving view the world and their future with confidence; they expect good things to happen and reframe negative events into learning experiences. As a result, they tend to be more satisfied with their lives and enjoy the college experience to a greater degree. Students with a positive perspective are able to take a long-term view of events and can see those events from multiple viewpoints. As a result, they experience positive emotions more frequently, which leads to higher levels of satisfaction with the college experience (Schreiner, Pothoven, Nelson, and McIntosh, 2009).

Congruent with the *positive relationships* dimension of Seligman's (2011) theory of well-being, *Social Connectedness* includes having good friends, being in relationship with others who listen to them, and feeling connected to others so that one is not lonely. As Seligman notes, "very little that is positive is solitary" (p. 20).

Diverse Citizenship reflects the desire to make a contribution to one's community as well as the confidence to do so; it reflects Seligman's (2011) component of *meaning* in his theory of well-being. Thriving students take the time to help others, responding to them with openness and curiosity. They want to make a difference in their community and to society (Schreiner, McIntosh, Nelson, and Pothoven, 2009), a goal that is consistent with the civic engagement objectives that have historically characterized higher education.

Pathways to Thriving: One Size Does Not Fit All

In research conducted across a broad cross-section of college students in the United States, Canada, and Australia, students' scores on the Thriving Quotient were significantly predictive of the outcomes higher education tends to value most, adding 12 to 23 percent to the variation in grade point average (GPA), intent to graduate, institutional fit, satisfaction, perception of tuition worth, and learning gains (Schreiner, Pothoven, and others, 2009). Students' characteristics at the time of entry into college, long the staple of higher education regression analyses, were insignificant predictors of these outcomes once their thriving levels were taken into account. Even race/ethnicity no longer contributed any predictive value to student success outcomes—good news indeed, as such demographic characteristics are not aspects of the student experience that can be changed.

We also have found that students' scores on the Thriving Quotient could be reliably predicted by the quality of their experiences on campus;

however, students' entering characteristics were significantly predictive of their thriving levels as well (Schreiner, Kammer, Primrose, and Quick, 2011). Although student thriving was influenced by a number of factors, the magnitude of these effects differed greatly across ethnicities. In essence, evidence suggests that there is not one pathway to thriving for all college students; there are many different pathways that vary depending on a student's ethnicity.

A focus on thriving as a more holistic view of student success holds considerable potential for addressing the pervasive gaps in educational attainment across ethnic groups that have characterized the last three decades of American higher education (Hennessy, 2010). As historically underrepresented groups are the fastest-growing demographic in U.S. higher education, Hurtado and colleagues (2012) remind us that "we are at a critical crossroad—the success of diverse college students is tied to our collective social and economic success" (p. 42).

Students of color experience predominantly White campuses in significantly different ways than their Caucasian counterparts (Fischer, 2007; Hurtado and Ponjuan, 2005; Perna and Thomas, 2006). For example, ethnic minority students' satisfaction and sense of belonging on campus are typically lower than what White students report (Park, 2009), their relationships with faculty are qualitatively different and contribute differently to their learning gains (Cole, 2007; Lundberg and Schreiner, 2004), and their process of adjustment to college differs, along with the role that campus involvement plays in their success (Fischer, 2007).

Of particular interest to student affairs professionals are three specific contributors to thriving in White students that may be experienced quite differently by students of color: campus involvement, spirituality, and sense of community. These diverse pathways to thriving indicate that there are particular areas of campus programming that can be targeted to enhance the connection that students feel to the university, thereby impacting their institutional commitment and likelihood of success.

Campus Involvement. Astin's (1984) theory of involvement has long held that investment of physical and psychological energy on campus produces learning gains, as well as many other benefits for students. However, researchers have found mixed results on the role that such involvement plays in the lives of students of color. For example, Fischer (2007) found that African American and Latino students' adjustment to college benefited greatly from formal campus involvement, but Lundberg, Schreiner, Hovaguimian, and Slavin Miller (2007) found that although African American students participate more in campus activities, they report fewer learning gains from that involvement than other students.

In research on the contribution of campus involvement to student thriving across ethnic groups, we have found that such involvement benefited African American students least, except in cases where the involvement was in ethnic organizations. Latino students benefited most from campus involvement, although participation in ethnic organizations did not contribute significantly to their thriving. Caucasian and Asian American students also benefited from campus involvement, although for these students their involvement contributed most when it was accompanied by student-faculty interaction (Schreiner, Kammer, Primrose, and Quick, 2011). Thus, the simplistic solution of "more involvement" in order to help students thrive does not adequately reflect the important nuances in the types of involvement that contribute most to thriving.

Student affairs professionals are well positioned to help students become selectively involved in the campus activities and organizations most likely to connect to their passions, identities, and interests. This selective involvement appears to be a crucial ingredient in the contribution of involvement to thriving, as too much involvement can detract from other commitments, and participating in events that are not likely to enhance a sense of belonging can be counterproductive.

Another key strategy for student affairs professionals is to not only solicit input from a wide array of students in planning campus events and activities, but to encourage diverse groups of students to plan and implement the programming so that it meets the needs of more students and encourages ownership. Involvement per se is not the answer; involvement in meaningful and rewarding activities that embrace the contribution of each participant is what leads to thriving.

Spirituality. Connecting intellect and spirit has not received much recognition in the higher education literature until recently (Astin, Astin, and Lindholm, 2011; Bryant and Astin, 2008), yet such a connection can lead to distinct benefits for students, ranging from learning gains to satisfaction with their entire college experience (Astin, Astin, and Lindholm, 2011; Kuh and Gonyea, 2006). Spirituality can often be an effective internal coping mechanism as well, as it is associated with a positive perspective on the world (Koenig, 2001).

Astin and colleagues' (2011) landmark national longitudinal study defines spirituality as "our sense of who we are and where we come from, our beliefs about why we are here—the meaning and purpose that we see in our work and our life—our sense of connectedness to one another and to the world around us" (p. 4). In their study, students with higher spirituality scores were more satisfied with college, received higher grades, were more likely to embrace diversity, and exhibited higher academic self-esteem.

Spirituality may serve different functions in people's lives, however, and as such differs across ethnic groups. For example, qualitative studies of African American students on predominantly White campuses have found that spirituality is a lens used to interpret and make sense of their identities (Stewart, 2009) and is perceived as important in overcoming life's challenges (Constantine and others, 2006). Walker and Dixon's (2002) correlational study found a significant relationship between academic success and reliance on a higher power among African American students. Latino students report greater levels of religious engagement (Campesino, Belyea, and Schwartz, 2009), and their spirituality and faith practices are linked with healthy psychological well-being (Cervantes and Parham, 2005).

Levels of spirituality have been found to differ across ethnic groups (Parks, 2000); in our studies, spirituality also contributed differentially to student thriving. For example, there were no direct effects of spirituality on Latino thriving levels, yet spirituality had a substantial effect on thriving in Asian American and African American students and a moderate effect in Caucasian students (Schreiner, Kammer, and others, 2011). As Rockenbach and Mayhew (2012) have found, the role of spirituality differs in the lives of students from different cultural backgrounds; as such, its contribution to student thriving also differs by ethnicity.

Student affairs professionals' awareness of the differing importance of spirituality in students' lives can result in campus programming that provides sacred spaces as well as culturally appropriate religious observances and opportunities. In addition, professionals can structure spiritual support systems on campus to best meet the needs of the diverse students. For example, opportunities for religious engagement may be important to some students, whereas spiritual needs may be more closely related to coping mechanisms, opportunities to discuss the big questions of life, or interacting with other students from similar backgrounds and traditions.

As student affairs professionals create campus programming that takes into consideration these different pathways to thriving, it is critical to recognize that one size does not fit all. Despite this need for customization, foundational to any efforts to enhance college student thriving is the ability to create a sense of community on campus.

Creating a Sense of Community on Campus: The Foundation for Thriving

Creating a sense of community on campus is the single best way to help all students thrive. Defined as "a feeling that members have of belonging and being important to each other, and a shared faith that their needs will be met by their commitment to be together" (McMillan and Chavis, 1986, p. 9), sense of community encompasses feelings of ownership and belonging, emotional connections with others in the community, and interdependent partnerships. This sense of belonging to something larger than oneself—feeling connected and valued—is a basic human need (Strayhorn, 2012). The failure to address this need on university campuses may be at least one of the reasons for the continuing disparity in success rates across ethnic and income groups, as it may be difficult to attend to academic tasks and challenges when this basic need remains unmet. As complex as the solutions may be, creating a sense of community on campus holds the greatest

Figure 4.2. Elements of a Psychological Sense of Community

Membership	Relationship
Sense of belonging and validation Symbols, signs, rituals, traditions	Shared emotional connection Opportunities for positive interactions
Ownership	Partnership
Student voice and contribution Mattering to the institution	Interdependence Shared goals

promise for making the kind of difference in students' lives that will help them thrive.

The four key elements of a sense of community include membership, ownership, relationship, and partnership (Schreiner, 2010b; see Figure 4.2). Students who report a strong sense of community on campus feel they are part of and contribute to a stable and dependable network of people who care about them, are committed to their growth and well-being, and are able to meet their needs (Lounsbury and DeNeui, 1995). They perceive the institution as committed to their welfare, delivering on its promises, and providing an appropriate space to connect to others in meaningful ways (Braxton, Hirschy, and McClendon, 2004). In our research on the different pathways to thriving across ethnic groups, a sense of community was the largest contributor to thriving for all students, but its predictive power varied by ethnicity, as did the campus experiences that influenced a sense of community (Schreiner, Kammer, Primrose, and Quick, 2011).

For example, involvement in campus activities was the strongest contributor to Latino students' sense of community, while for African American students it was spirituality. For Asian American students, sense of community came from their major, and for Caucasian students it was most influenced by interaction with faculty. So what can we do differently on our campuses if we want all students to thrive?

First, a sense of community involves *membership*—a sense of belonging, of feeling at home. Membership matters most when one is new to a community and when one is feeling marginalized. Membership is the foundation of a sense of community, for it implies that one has a rightful place in that community (Strayhorn, 2012). Yet as one Latino student said to me in discussing what it meant for a campus to be welcoming, "even the word *welcome* implies that this is your house and you are inviting me in as a guest. An invited and welcome guest, for sure, but still a guest. I'm not part of the family."

Institutions that want to create a greater sense of community on campus must start with the sense of belonging and determine how to communicate it to all students (Hurtado and Carter, 1997). Rendon (1994) emphasizes validation—actions that faculty and staff take to empower students and communicate that they are capable learners who have a contribution to make. Hurtado and colleagues (2012) note that these messages from faculty are most influential with students of color when they are interpersonal forms of validation, rather than academic in nature.

Staff are also in a key position to validate students. As institutional agents, they may be more strategically influential in students' lives during times of transition. Thus, developing the validating skills of faculty and staff may be one way to create a stronger sense of community on campus.

Ownership is the second dimension of a sense of community, involving voice and contribution. Students who feel a sense of ownership believe that they are valued by the community and that their input matters. Braxton, Hirschy, and McClendon (2004) refer to this element as a "commitment of the institution to student welfare" (p. 22). This commitment is best conveyed through the signals that the university sends to students in its messages and policies. Institutions can regularly seek student input through annual satisfaction surveys, focus groups, and designating students as regular members of university committees.

Input and involvement from diverse students is particularly important in planning and implementing campus events and activities, as our research demonstrates that campus involvement does not engender a sense of community equally across all ethnic groups (Schreiner, Kammer, Primrose, and Quick, 2011). Keeping the university "psychologically small," through small living units, reasonable class sizes, and small work units for faculty and staff, can enhance the sense of ownership as each member of the community feels valued and believes that his or her input makes a difference.

The third dimension of a sense of community is *relationship*. Positive relationships with others on campus create a strong emotional connection that builds a sense of community. Although many universities orient their first-year programming toward this task, research demonstrates that the sophomore year may be just as critical in helping students connect to others and develop relationships (Schaller, 2010). Campus involvement is one way to build relationships, but that involvement must be selective and geared toward students' interests, passions, and needs, while not interfering with academic or work commitments—a tall order! Conducting regular needs assessments of students on campus, including a wide variety of students on planning teams for campus events, and regularly assessing campus programming to determine if there was a differential impact on certain kinds of students can help student development staff facilitate the kind of involvement on campus that will enable more students to thrive.

Learning communities, whether they are living-learning facilities in residence halls or blocks of courses taught by a team of faculty, enhance the development of positive relationships and represent a high-impact educational practice advocated by the Association of American Colleges and Universities (AACU) (Kuh, 2008) and other professional organizations. Student Life staff can play a vital role in the development of these communities as they partner with faculty to design a wide variety of options where diverse students can interact with one another and with faculty on a regular basis, forming a community committed to mutual learning goals.

The final component of a sense of community is *partnership,* expressed as mutual goals that require collaboration with others in order to succeed. Examples of such partnerships include team-based learning in the classroom, student-faculty research projects, and service-learning opportunities, as well as internships and cooperative education with local organizations and businesses. An entire campus may come together toward a particularly large and meaningful goal—such as supporting a local school or homeless shelter—with various groups on campus contributing out of their strengths: athletic teams planning recreational events; theater and music groups organizing entertainment; allied health majors sponsoring a wellness fair; business majors marketing the event; and student government managing the logistics and budget. As students contribute individually toward the success of the partnership, they also experience themselves as an integral part of the community, people whose needs are being met and who are meeting the needs of others.

This type of community is also a place where faculty, staff, and administrators enjoy working, as they are part of the meaningful enterprise of "growing students." When campus personnel feel valued for the work they do and see it as an important contribution to the life of the community, these positive emotions will translate to greater care and concern for students. When students experience the campus community as a safe place where they belong and are valued, where they experience positive emotional connections and matter to others, and where they believe they have something to contribute and their needs will be met, they are highly likely to thrive—socially, emotionally, and academically.

References

Astin, A. W. "Student Involvement: A Developmental Theory for Higher Education." *Journal of College Student Personnel, 25,* 1984, 297–308.
Astin, A. W., Astin, H. S., and Lindholm, J. A. *Cultivating the Spirit: How College Can Enhance Students' Inner Lives.* San Francisco: Jossey-Bass, 2011.

Bean, J. P., and Eaton, S. B. "A Psychological Model of College Student Retention." In J. M. Braxton (ed.), *Reworking the Student Departure Puzzle* (pp. 48–61). Nashville, Tenn.: Vanderbilt University Press, 2000.

Berger, J. B., and Milem, J. F. "The Role of Student Involvement and Perceptions of Integration in a Causal Model of Student Persistence." *Research in Higher Education*, 1999, *40*, 641–664.

Braxton, J. M., Hirschy, A. S., and McClendon, S. A. *Understanding and Reducing College Student Departure*. ASHE-ERIC Higher Education Report *30*(3). San Francisco: Wiley, 2004.

Bryant, A. N., and Astin, H. S. "The Correlates of Spiritual Struggle During the College Years." *Journal of Higher Education*, 2008, *79*(1), 1–27. doi: 10.1353/jhe.2008.0000

Campesino, M., Belyea, M., and Schwartz, G. "Spirituality and Cultural Identification Among Latino and Non-Latino College Students. *Hispanic Health Care International*, 2009, *7*(2), 1–13.

Cervantes, J. M., and Parham, T. A. "Toward a Meaningful Spirituality for People of Color: Lessons for the Counseling Practitioner." *Cultural Diversity and Ethnic Minority Psychology*, 2005, *11*(1), 69–81.

Cole, D. "Do Interracial Interactions Matter? An Examination of Student-Faculty Contact and Intellectual Self-Concept." *Journal of Higher Education*, 2007, *78*(3), 249–281. doi: 10.1353/jhe.2007.0015

Constantine, M. G., and others. "Religion, Spirituality, and Career Development in African American College Students: A Qualitative Inquiry." *Career Development Quarterly*, 2006, *54*(3), 227–241.

Fischer, M. "Settling into Campus Life: Differences by Race/Ethnicity in College Involvement and Outcomes." *Journal of Higher Education*, 2007, *78*(2), 125–161.

Hennessy, E. *New Data Indicate Educational Attainment Continues to Flat-Line*. American Council on Education, 2010. Retrieved from http://www.acenet.eduhttp://www.acenet.edu/

Hurtado, S., and others. "A Model for Diverse Learning Environments." In J. C. Smart and M. B. Paulsen (eds.), *Higher Education: Handbook of Theory and Research* (vol. 27, pp. 41–122). Dordrecht, Netherlands: Springer, 2012.

Hurtado, S., and Carter, D. F. "Effects of College Transition and Perceptions of the Campus Racial Climate on Latino College Students' Sense of Belonging." *Sociology of Education*, 1997, *70*(4), 324–345.

Hurtado, S., and Ponjuan, L. "Latino Educational Outcomes and the Campus Climate." *Journal of Hispanic Education*, 2005, *4*(3), 235–251. doi: 10.1177/1538192705276548

Keyes, C. L. M. "Complete Mental Health: an Agenda for the 21st Century." In C. L. M. Keyes and J. Haidt (eds.), *Flourishing: Positive Psychology and the Life Well-Lived* (pp. 293–309). Washington, D.C.: American Psychological Association, 2003.

Keyes, C.L.M., and Haidt, J. (eds.). *Flourishing: Positive Psychology and the Life Well-Lived*. Washington, D.C.: American Psychological Association, 2003.

Koenig, H. G. "Religion and medicine II: Religion, mental health, and related behaviors." *International Journal of Psychiatry in Medicine*, 2001, *31*(1), 97–109.

Kuh, G. D. *High-Impact Educational Practices: What They Are, Who Has Access to Them, and Why They Matter*. Washington, D.C.: American Association of Colleges and Universities, 2008.

Kuh, G. D., and Gonyea, R. M. "Spirituality, Liberal Learning, and College Student Engagement." *Liberal Education*, 2006, *92*(1), 40–47.

Lopez, S. J., and Louis, M. C. "The Principles of Strengths-Based Education." *Journal of College and Character*, 2009, *10*(4), 1–8.

Lounsbury, J. W., and DeNeui, D. "Psychological Sense of Community on Campus." *College Student Journal*, 1995, *29*(3), 270–277.

Lundberg, C. A., and Schreiner, L. A. "Quality and Frequency of Faculty-Student Interaction as Predictors of Learning: an Analysis by Student Race/Ethnicity." *Journal of College Student Development,* 2004, *45*(5), 549–565.

Lundberg, C. A., Schreiner, L. A., Hovaguimian, K. D., and Slavin Miller, S. "First-Generation Status and Student Race/Ethnicity as Distinct Predictors of Student Involvement and Learning." *NASPA Journal,* 2007, *44*(1), 57–83.

McMillan, D. W., and Chavis, D. M. "Sense of Community: A Definition and Theory." *Journal of Community Psychology,* 1986, *14,* 6–23.

Park, J. J. "Are We Satisfied? a Look at Student Satisfaction with Diversity at Traditionally White Institutions." *Review of Higher Education,* 2009, *32*(3), 291–320.

Parks, S. D. Big Questions, Worthy Dreams: Mentoring Young Adults in Their Search for Meaning, Purpose and Faith. San Francisco: Jossey-Bass, 2000.

Perna, L. W., and Thomas, S. L. "A Framework for Reducing the College Success Gap and Promoting Success for All." Commissioned report for the National Symposium on Postsecondary Student Success: Spearheading a Dialog on Student Success, 2006.

Pintrich, P. R. "A Conceptual Framework for Assessing Motivation and Self-Regulated Learning in College Students." *Educational Psychology Review,* 2004, *16*(4), 385–407.

Rendon, L. I. "Validating Culturally Diverse Students: Toward a New Model for Learning and Student Development." *Innovative Higher Education,* 1994, *27*(4), 235–252.

Robbins, S. B., and others. "Do Psychosocial and Study Skill Factors Predict College Outcomes? A Meta-Analysis." *Psychological Bulletin,* 2004, *130,* 261–288.

Rockenbach, A. B., and Mayhew, M. J. (eds.). *Spirituality in College Students' Lives: Translating Research into Practice.* New York: Routledge, 2012.

Ryff, C. D., and Keyes, C. L. M. "The Structure of Psychological Well-Being Revisited." *Journal of Personality and Social Psychology,* 1995, *69,* 719–727, 1995.

Schaller, M. A. "College Sophomores: The Journey into Self." In M. Hunter and others (eds.), *Helping Sophomores Succeed: Understanding and Improving the Second-Year Experience* (pp. 66–81). San Francisco: Jossey-Bass, 2010.

Schreiner, L. "The 'Thriving Quotient': A New Vision for Student Success." *About Campus,* 2010a, *15*(2), 2–10.

Schreiner, L. "Thriving in Community." *About Campus,* 2010b, *15*(4), 2–11.

Schreiner, L., Kammer, R., Primrose, B., and Quick, D. "Predictors of Thriving in Students of Color: Differential Pathways to College Success." Paper presented at the annual meeting of the Association for the Study of Higher Education, Charlotte, NC, 2011.

Schreiner, L., and Louis, M. "The Engaged Learning Index: Implications for Faculty Development." *Journal on Excellence in College Teaching,* 2011, *22*(1), 5–28.

Schreiner, L., McIntosh, E., Nelson, D., and Pothoven, S. "The Thriving Quotient: Advancing the Assessment of Student Success." Paper presented at the annual meeting of the Association for the Study of Higher Education, Vancouver, British Columbia, November 2009.

Schreiner, L., Pothoven, S., Nelson, D., and McIntosh, E. "College Student Thriving: Predictors of Success and Retention." Paper presented at the annual meeting of the Association for the Study of Higher Education, Vancouver, British Columbia, November 2009.

Seligman, M.E.P. *Flourish: A Visionary New Understanding of Happiness and Well-Being.* New York: Free Press, 2011.

Stewart, D. L. "Perceptions of Multiple Identities Among Black College Students." *Journal of College Student Development,* 2009, *50*(3), 253–270.

Strayhorn, T. L. *College Students' Sense of Belonging: A Key to Educational Success for All Students.* New York: Routledge, 2012.

Tagg, J. *The Learning Paradigm College*. Bolton: Anker, 2003.

Walker, K. L., and Dixon, V. "Spirituality and Academic Performance Among African American College Students." *Journal of Black Psychology,* 2002, 28(2), 107–121.

LAURIE SCHREINER is professor and chair of the doctoral programs in higher education at Azusa Pacific University.

5

This chapter describes the results of a study that provides a rich understanding of the role of curiosity in facilitating academic and personal success in high-achieving college students.

Fostering Student Engagement by Cultivating Curiosity

Eileen Hulme, Daniel T. Green, Kimberly S. Ladd

Student engagement with professors, peers, intellectually challenging subject matter, and supportive environments has been identified repeatedly as a significant factor facilitating students' success in college. The time and effort a student expends on his or her educational pursuits are positively related to academic outcomes such as grade point average and first-to-second-year retention (Kuh and others, 2008). However, many colleges and universities continue to experience low retention and graduation rates as well as indications of limited academic gains (Arum and Roska, 2010). As institutions have struggled to understand the factors that affect engagement and retention, research on noncognitive variables (e.g., achievement motivation, academic self-efficacy, and emotional intelligence) has proliferated over the past ten years. The fact that some students from the same educational and socioeconomic backgrounds succeed and others fail remains a significant unanswered question for the higher education community compelled to improve retention and graduation rates.

The emerging field of positive psychology has provided a new perspective on the existing retention problem plaguing higher education by identifying curiosity as one of the character strengths that influence a person's drive and ultimately their level of academic engagement. Along with hope, self-determination, and a zest for living, curiosity has been identified as a character trait that correlates with high levels of student satisfaction and academic success (Lounsbury, Fisher, Levy, and Welsh, 2009). Therefore, as colleges and universities focus on improving both curricular and co-curricular engagement, higher education leaders should examine how to create environments that may best nurture a student's level of curiosity.

NEW DIRECTIONS FOR STUDENT SERVICES, no. 143, Fall 2013 © Wiley Periodicals, Inc.
Published online in Wiley Online Library (wileyonlinelibrary.com) • DOI: 10.1002/ss.20060

This chapter provides an overview of the nuances of curiosity as well as exploring the ramifications of a new study, "Curiosity in High-Achieving College Students" (Hulme and others, 2012), which supports the assertion that curiosity is common among highly engaged students. Additionally, the study's findings provide a road map for institutions interested in engaging the spirit of exploration within their students.

Curiosity as the Foundation for Student Engagement

Defined as a willingness to explore the unknown, embrace novelty, and accept uncertainty, curiosity has been shown to have a significant effect on motivation and learning (Kashdan, Rose, and Finchman, 2004). Silvia (2006) determined that when people experience curiosity they learn in deeper and more meaningful ways with better retention of the information they are studying. They concentrate more fully, and persevere until they meet their goals. Harachkiewicz, Barron, Tauer, and Elliot (2002) concluded that greater curiosity-related behaviors and cognitions are associated with improved learning, engagement, and performance in academic settings. Curiosity has a significant positive relationship with constructs that impact learning such as emotional intelligence (Leonard and Harvey, 2007), and intrinsic motivation (Ryan and Deci, 2000; Tsai and others, 2008). Additionally, one's level of curiosity has a beneficial effect on social intimacy, health, sense of purpose, and overall happiness (Kashdan, 2009).

Theorists argue that curious individuals possess the desire to explore and seek out new knowledge and experiences. They constantly search for novelty even in the familiar (Ainley, 1987; Berlyne, 1960; Pearson, 1970). Curious individuals are constantly searching for novelty even in the familiar.

Also, theorists propose that curiosity is shaped by the willingness to delve into uncertainty and unpredictability (Berg and Sternberg, 1985; Silvia, 2008). An overreliance on expert opinions to create the appearance of certainty diminishes the need and desire for mindful exploration (Langer, 1997), thus potentially reducing curiosity.

Emerging Research on Curiosity in High-Achieving College Students

Silvia's (2006) work on the effect of curiosity on the learning process provides a compelling reason for colleges and universities to focus on developing this trait. Additionally, more recent studies have begun to indicate that curiosity is closely linked to the success of high-achieving students. Louis and Hulme (2012) conducted a qualitative study of Truman Scholars to determine the distinguishing characteristics, attitudes, and strengths of high-achieving college students. The prestigious Truman scholarship is a highly competitive award given to college juniors who demonstrate leadership potential, perform well academically, and express a desire to pursue careers in public service (http://www.truman.gov). The rigorous Truman selection process ensured a qualified, national sample for the study.

Two overarching themes emerged from the data to become the foundation for the development of a grounded theory (Louis and Hulme, 2012). The high-achieving students in the sample demonstrated an unquenchable curiosity toward their academic pursuits and a passionate drive toward their goals. Their curiosity and passion enabled them to rise above their fear of failure, live with uncertainty, and engage in purposeful activities. However, focusing solely on Truman Scholars created a sample that overly represented students from highly selective universities. Additional studies were needed to include high-achieving students from more diverse institutions.

The Study of High-Achieving College Students

Because of the need for more data, in August 2012, academics at five universities commenced a one-year study entitled, "Curiosity in High-Achieving College Students." Using a grounded theory qualitative approach, the study illustrates curiosity's place in academic and personal success in high-achieving college students at the end of their undergraduate college careers. For the purposes of this study, a student was considered high achieving if he or she had a GPA of 3.8 or higher and held a significant leadership (e.g., student government office or student organization president) role on campus. The study sample consisted of 20 students from five different universities located in five different states.

Two rounds of semistructured interviews with college seniors were conducted to understand the nature and nuances of curiosity. Each interview explored the student's perspectives on attitudes and behaviors that reflected exploration and environments that supported the development of greater levels of curiosity. In the second interview, the themes that emerged from the first interview were pursued in more detail. The data were analyzed using open, axial, and selective coding.

The Bifurcation of Exploration: Mastery Versus Performance

Throughout the interview process, it became evident that curiosity manifested itself through a student's desire to explore. However, motivation for exploration took two distinct paths based on an individual's orientation toward learning. Students demonstrated a desire to learn for the sake of increasing knowledge (mastery orientation) or to learn for the purpose of reaching an externally established standard (performance orientation). Those on the path of exploration for the sake of mastery sought to expand and deepen their knowledge about a subject or activity. These students asked questions because they were interested in learning for learning's sake.

They explored an academic subject or engaged in co-curricular pursuits out of a true desire to master a topic or activity. Students on the mastery path expressed broad, deep interests. Students who were performance-oriented tended to have a more focused approach to learning. These students studied and sought information from the professor; however, they often stated that they were more likely to explore topics that would improve their performance in class. They utilized their curiosity to explore information that would result in a good grade or extrinsic reward.

Students interviewed for the "Curiosity in High-Achieving College Students" study often exhibited a combination of both mastery and performance traits; however, one particular orientation was consistently more prevalent in their attitudes and behaviors. This finding mirrors the work of achievement goal theorists who delineate between performance and mastery goals. Performance goals are based on a person's desire to outperform others (performance approach) or the fear of being out performed by others (performance avoidance). Mastery goals are based in individuals' desires to better themselves (for reviews, see Elliot, 2005; Pintrich and Schunk, 2002). We found a clear link between individual experiences of curiosity and goal orientation. Within this framework, we discovered five areas that affected our participants' level of curiosity in an academic setting: intellectual challenge, approach to uncertainty, relationship to fear of failure, search for meaning and purpose, and dimensions of psychosocial support.

Intellectual Challenge. Students with a strong sense of curiosity actively seek opportunities for new information and experiences (Ainley, 1987; Berlyne, 1960). The manner in which a student approached intellectually challenging material within a course demonstrated the difference between those with a performance or mastery orientation. The students with a performance orientation were primarily concerned with their classroom performance as measured by grades, instructor feedback, and the successful completion of the course. Many reported that "getting the class out of the way" was their primary objective. Likewise, students evaluated their co-curricular performances according to how their actions would elicit recognition from peers or enhance recognition from future employers. Their curiosity was limited by their desire to "provide faculty members what they wanted."

Students who possessed a mastery orientation recognized their role in the co-creation of knowledge within the classroom. They framed information being presented so that it related to their current reality. They demonstrated a high level of intrinsic motivation and they expressed a desire to be intellectually challenged. One participant, frustrated with the lack of demanding coursework, stated, "I think we kill curiosity by being too nice. I think that's the biggest downfall of my education. Every professor that I've had is too nice. I feel like I shouldn't have straight A's in every class." It appears from this study that highly curious students long to be challenged to explore at increasingly deeper levels of complexity.

NEW DIRECTIONS FOR STUDENT SERVICES • DOI: 10.1002/ss

Approach to Uncertainty. Individuals who are naturally curious embrace the uncertain aspects of life (Kashdan, 2009). They tend not to be deterred by a lack of understanding or prior experience. By examining the nature of the questions students asked, a clear delineation between the mastery- and performance-oriented students emerged. Those with a performance focus tended to ask questions to find a specific answer and therefore eliminate uncertainty. These students would often ask a question with the intention of receiving a definitive answer, so they could move on and address the next problem presented in class. Those with a mastery orientation asked questions to expand their knowledge. They routinely developed new questions to ask because they thrived on creating uncertainty for themselves. One participant stated:

> When I'm curious about something, I seek people out who I think have different perspectives on something that I'm curious about. For me it is being willing to ask questions and then when you walk away, thinking through what you've been told and coming up with new questions. I will never run out of questions because I'm constantly longing for more information.

In addition, a mastery orientation compelled students to take more risks in their co-curricular experiences. They readily saw the opportunity to grow by pushing themselves into unfamiliar places. Traveling to foreign countries and joining diverse groups demonstrated their willingness to embrace new experiences. A mastery orientation appears to expand a student's level of curiosity, which results in a greater motivation to incur risks. Students with a performance orientation were less likely to move toward uncertainty unless there was an obvious extrinsic reward that they highly valued that was associated with the action. Therefore, it appears that students with a performance orientation tend to avoid risk. One student with a general performance orientation stated: "I'm kind of risk averse. It's actually funny because I have these talks with my best friend here all the time, and he's extremely risk averse, too. So we just talk about where we want to be and how we're going to get there." Therefore, the results from the study indicated that the highly curious students interviewed enjoyed experiences that required them to confront existing paradigms. Additionally, they appeared to be comfortable living with the ambiguity of uncertainty.

Relationship to Fear of Failure. Students' willingness to embrace uncertainty appeared to have a deep connection with their outlook on failure. Those with the performance orientation appeared to avoid situations in which they might fail. Seemingly, these students' identities were aligned with how successful or unsuccessful they were in their actions. If they thought they might fail, it influenced their decision-making ability and ultimately their levels of curiosity. One participant said, "I don't try to do the things I won't be successful at." Another participant stated, "I did a lot of sports growing up and if I didn't know how to get better or if I just failed, I was done." Some performance-oriented students used their fear of failure as motivation to push themselves. One stated: "I think that it's very valuable, especially for my motivation habits to be driven by the fear of failure." The performance-oriented students' levels of curiosity did not seem to compel them beyond the parameters of their perceived abilities.

Many of those with the mastery orientation viewed failure as an opportunity to improve. They reframed their failures by emphasizing the perceived learning gains thus engendering a more pervasive sense of curiosity. One participant mentioned: "Sometimes what we perceive as a failure is just another way to learn for the future. I think it depends on how we're looking at it. Bring it on. I think it's humbling and sometimes I need that. So humble me, but not too much." Those with a mastery orientation were less likely to define their abilities based on failure or success. They recognized and embraced the struggle to not allow failure to define them. One participant noted the struggle when she stated: "The most important thing is to not be afraid of failure and that's hard to accept especially if you're an achiever." Embracing uncertainty and reframing failures were certainly two aspects that defined a student whose curiosity was shaped by a mastery orientation. However, it appeared that the deepest motivation toward exploration was found within a student's sense of purpose.

Meaning and Purpose. Frankl (1985) theorized that finding purpose and meaning in life is the central motivating force in all individuals. Students, in this study, described the discovery of purpose as "following their passions." They appeared to experience greater levels of curiosity when they were pursuing those classes and activities that related to their personal passion or purpose in life. However, students who were more oriented toward performance often equated meaning and purpose with the grades they earned. They found purpose in the act of meeting other's expectations, achieving visible leadership positions, or maintaining a high GPA. Whereas students with a strong mastery orientation explored things they were passionate about regardless of extrinsic rewards. Their drive to explore went hand-in-hand with pursuing subjects and activities that provided meaning and purpose. One participant described the relationship between learning and a sense of purpose when he stated: "I ended up choosing International Business because I wanted to find ways that I could serve God and help those in need through business and how I could help them now by creating jobs." It appears from the study that curiosity exhibited by both performance and mastery-oriented students is clearly linked to a sense of purpose and meaning. However, the pathways to determining and achieving their passions in life were significantly different depending on their orientation.

The Effect of Psychosocial Support Systems. Another area that shaped a participant's willingness to explore had to do with the student's psychosocial support systems. Researchers have established how a student's support system can provide him or her with a sense of belonging, and enhance one's value in relating to others or to one's self (Astin, 1993;

Chickering and Reisser, 1993). The psychological development in, and interaction with, their social environment shaped participants' level of curiosity. The students in the study reported that faculty, student affairs staff, and parents had a significant effect on their desire to take either a mastery or performance approach to exploration.

As participant's described their academic experiences it became clear that faculty members themselves either had a performance or mastery orientation to their pedagogy. Performance-oriented faculty members would often lecture to the test. One participant quoted a professor who simply stated before a test, "Here's what you need to know, so memorize it!" Another student recalled a professor stating, "I want the average on this test to be a 70." Participants stated that the more performance-oriented faculty members often gave multiple-choice tests rather than requiring critical thinking from the students. Faculty members who demonstrated a mastery orientation were more likely to ask open-ended questions and exhibit a passion for their subject through their own curiosity. One student, when describing a mastery-oriented faculty member stated, "My professor doesn't like settling for just one source. I think her passion has helped me find my own passion and that it's okay to ask questions." However, the manner in which students reacted to such an educator was markedly different based on their own orientation.

Performance-orientated students seemed to resonate with performance-oriented teachers who clearly outlined how to receive an A in class and valued their desire to meet the stated requirements. Even when several of the students expressed a natural curiosity about the subject matter, if the faculty member had a performance orientation, they were more likely to emphasize the importance of taking the necessary steps in order to achieve a good grade in the class.

In contrast, students with a high-mastery orientation praised those professors who were passionate about the subject being taught or teachers who encouraged exploration. These students cited examples in which they were encouraged to take chances despite the risk of receiving a lesser grade. One student stated: "The professor would push you to the point where he knew he was challenging you. You really felt you learned something or you had struggled through an idea and understood it better. That personalized pushing you to your limit academically was really interesting. I enjoyed it." When a mastery-oriented student had a performance-oriented faculty member, they often found ways to make the material personally meaningful and searched for opportunities to explore the material in more depth. Mastery-oriented students appeared to be more comfortable with the professor introducing topics that were more ambiguous or created feelings of uncertainty.

Several students reported that their involvement in co-curricular activities was a positive influence in their college careers. The students specifically cited how student affairs professionals positively affected their level of confidence, encouraging them to seek out new experiences throughout their college experience. However, the data did not reveal a clear distinction between how mastery- and performance-oriented students experienced this support. Both types of participants stated that staff members took an interest in their development and encouraged them to take on leadership roles even if the student did not feel ready to take on more responsibility. One participant acknowledged this encouragement that the staff provided: "The only reason why I am capable of taking on as much as I am is because I have people who are encouraging it. The university appreciates students who are not strictly academically focused." The student responses appear to indicate that the support they found through co-curricular involvement enabled them to deal with the uncertainty of exploration. One student simply stated: "I have people who are there who are encouraging me to explore."

One of the strongest influences on the high-achieving participants had to do with parental support. Participants who stated that their parents defined success in college by a high grade point average gravitated toward a performance orientation. These students were more likely to indicate that their parents had placed a great deal of pressure on them to succeed. Some participants felt that their worth was directly proportional to their grades. One woman stated: "If I made below a B, that was failure, even though that's kind of an average range, but I was the good child in the family. So if I stooped to my brother's level, what did my parents have?" Another participant, a first-generation Vietnamese woman in her early 20s, stated that her greatest academic influence was her father, even though he never finished high school.

> He always told me as a child I was capable and that I have access to all these things that he did not. There were always these running jokes, he won't be satisfied until one of his kids is president, and they were jokes, but we believed we were capable of these things. But I always get really choked up when I talk about my father though because I don't want to disappoint him.

For many performance-oriented students, the desire to not disappoint parents appeared to significantly shape how they experienced their college years.

Participants with the mastery orientation felt great support from parents and stated that they were given encouragement to grow as individuals. Some participants stated that parents did not inquire about grades when they saw them at the end of the semester, but instead asked about college experiences. One student stated that his mother encouraged him to think about why he was enrolled in a class. "One thing my mom always taught me was it wasn't about grades, it was about how much you learned. And so that's something that I've tried to keep in mind as I've gone through my college experience. Am I really learning what these quizzes are supposed to assess?" However, it is important to note that this study does not prove causality. It cannot be said that performance-oriented parents produce performance-oriented children. However, it does appear that the orientation of the students does affect what they remember from their childhood and how they translate that experience into their approach toward learning.

Practical Suggestions for Enhancing Curiosity Through Student Affairs Practice

As the study illustrates, faculty, parents, and staff have a significant effect on a student's goal orientation and their level of curiosity. Student affairs professionals and faculty members are positioned to promote a mastery-oriented curiosity. The following suggestions were either provided directly from students or emerged from relevant aspects of the study.

Student Affairs Professionals and Faculty Must Model Curiosity as a Way of Leading. Students are constantly watching the behaviors of those they hold in high regard as a means of shaping their own behaviors. Every day, student affairs administrators and faculty serve as role models for a new generation of leaders. To enable them to fully engage in a rapidly changing world, curiosity must be modeled. Therefore, administrators should consider their own orientation toward learning and evaluate their responses to uncertainty and failure. When failures are shared openly and viewed through the lens of a discovery opportunity, students begin to understand that there is value not only in the performance outcome but also in the learning process itself. Additionally, administrators should create opportunities to share the meaning they and others derive from their work. Too often, the tyranny of deadlines replaces thoughtful conversations about matters that make life purposeful. As administrators intentionally focus on their level of curiosity, it is possible that students' lives will be transformed as well.

Challenge Students to Conceptualize Failure as a Valuable Part of the Learning Process. The most important discoveries of our times have come as a result of testing, failing, and trying again. In fact, the heart of the scientific method is systematic experimentation. As previously noted, students with a performance orientation toward exploration are often riddled with the fear that they might not achieve expected outcomes. However, students who naturally gravitate toward mastery learning seem to be able to transcend their fears, enabling them to follow their passions. An important question facing educators is: "How do we emphasize the importance of failure in the discovery process without promoting careless attitudes that engender unnecessary failure?" Creating opportunities for reflecting on failed attempts is an essential element for producing greater levels of curiosity in students. Student affairs professionals and faculty must intentionally seek out students who have experienced some degree of failure, such as those who lost an election, were not chosen for a leadership position, failed an exam, or experienced the fracturing of an important relationship. They need to provide a supportive environment for the mental and emotional processing of the event. Professionals, who are willing to reveal their own failures, create the transparency necessary to enable students to move beyond the emotional barriers they often establish after a failure.

Allow Students to Experience Uncertainty by Not Providing Quick Solutions to Problems. Students with high levels of curiosity tend to have more tolerance for ambiguity and perceive difficulties as opportunities rather than threats (Kashdan, 2009). However, student affairs practitioners and faculty feel the pressure to be certain about issues that relate to their areas of responsibility and expertise. The tendency to be quick to answer questions, thereby demonstrating knowledge, undermines our students' motivation to explore. Every student, not simply high-achieving students, can develop a tolerance for uncertainty and ambiguity if those in positions of authority demonstrate the same behavior. Simply responding to students' questions with the phrase "I don't know, what do you think?" can inspire exploration and potentially begin to shift their attention from performance to mastery.

Orient Students to the Role of Curiosity in the College Experience. Colleges and universities that are intentional about the messages they deliver during the first six weeks of a student's college career, are more likely to impact student behavior especially when those messages are reinforced throughout their college career. Introducing new students to the concept of curiosity and the long-term benefits of developing a mastery orientation to their classes and activities may encourage them to approach their college experience with an open mind and a desire to explore. The personal stories of students who exhibit a high degree of curiosity may inspire the excitement that can be found in learning.

Develop an Emphasis on Discovering a Sense of Meaning in Life. The matter of helping students develop a sense of purpose is often defined as a conversation about careers, and is usually relegated to the final semester of a student's senior year. However, the search for purpose is not synonymous with career exploration; rather, it is central to every individual's search for a meaningful life. Emmons (2003) postulates: "A meaningful life is one that is characterized by a deep sense of purpose, a sense of inner conviction, and assurance that in spite of one's current plight, life has significance" (p. 138). Whether a student possesses a mastery or performance orientation, our study seemed to indicate that their level of curiosity was intricately intertwined with a search for their passions and purpose. From this qualitative study, it was impossible to determine whether a student's sense of purpose enlivened their curiosity or whether their curiosity gave them the motivation to seek out their purpose. Regardless of the directionality of effect, providing students the opportunities to thoughtfully reflect on the greater purpose behind their curricular and co-curricular activities is essential to the college experience. Formal training opportunities, such as resident assistant training or student worker orientation, and informal conversations about campus life, provide student affairs professionals the opportunities to ask questions related to the meaning students are deriving from their campus involvement.

These suggestions provide student affairs professionals and faculty the opportunities to help students develop a greater sense of curiosity throughout college. However, as stated earlier, curiosity is contagious and can only be truly taught by individuals who are willing to embrace novelty and risk-taking. The first step of any programmatic emphasis on curiosity must be to encourage each professional to develop his or her own unique interests.

Conclusion

Myriad studies show that curiosity is an important motivational component in the lives of university and college students. Our findings indicate that rather than shying away from challenges, curious students tend to pursue uncertainty, exhibit openness to discovery, and perform better in school. Developing curiosity in students may produce higher levels of engagement, thus increasing the desire to matriculate through the entire higher education experience.

References

Ainley, M. D. "The Factor Structure of Curiosity Measures: Breadth and Depth of Interest Curiosity Styles." *Australian Journal of Psychology*, 1987, *39*, 53–59.

Arum, R., and Roska, J. *Academically Adrift: Limited Learning on College Campuses*. Chicago: University of Chicago Press, 2010.

Astin, A. *What Matters in College: Four Critical Years Revisited*. San Francisco: Jossey-Bass, 1993.

Berg, C. A., and Sternberg, R. J. "Response to Novelty: Continuity Versus Discontinuity in the Developmental Course of Intelligence." *Advances in Child Development and Behavior*, 1985, *19*, 1–47.

Berlyne, D. E. *Conflict, Arousal, and Curiosity*. New York: McGraw-Hill, 1960.

Chickering, A. W., and Reisser, L. *Education and Identity*. San Francisco: Jossey-Bass, 1993.

Elliot, A. J. "A Conceptual History of the Achievement Goal Construct, 1993." In A. J. Elliot and C. Dweck (eds.), *Handbook of Competence and Motivation* (pp. 52–72). New York: Guilford Press, 2005.

Emmons, R. *The Psychology of Ultimate Concerns: Motivation and Spirituality in Personality*. New York: Guilford Press, 2003.

Frankl, V. E. *Man's Search for Meaning* (Rev. ed.). New York: Washington Square Press, 1985.

Harackiewicz, J.M., Barron, K.E., Tauer, J.M., and Elliot, A.J. "Predicting Success in College: A Longitudinal Study of Achievement Goals and Ability Measures as Predictors of Interest and Performance From Freshman Year Through Graduation." *Journal of Educational Psychology*, 2002, *94*, 562–575.

Hulme, E., and others. "Curiosity in High Achieving College Students." Unpublished, 2012.

Kashdan, T. *Curious? Discover the Missing Ingredient to a Fulfilling Life.* New York: HarperCollins, 2009.

Kashdan, T. B., Rose, P., and Fincham, F. D. "Curiosity and Exploration: Facilitating Positive Subjective Experiences and Personal Growth Opportunities." *Journal of Personality Assessment,* 2004, *82*(3), 291–305.

Kuh, G., and others. "Unmasking the Effects of Student Engagement on First Year College Grades and Persistence." *Journal of Higher Education,* 2008, *79,* 540–563.

Langer, E. *The Power of Mindful Learning.* Cambridge, Mass.: Da Capo Press, 1997.

Leonard, N. H., and Harvey, M. "The Trait of Curiosity as a Predictor of Emotional Intelligence." *Journal of Applied Social Psychology,* 2007, *37,* 1914–1929.

Louis, M. C., and Hulme, E. Thriving in the Senior-Year Transition. In L. A. Schreiner, M. C. Louis, and D. D. Nelson (eds.), *Thriving in Transitions: A Research-Based Approach to College Student Success* (pp. 167–190). Columbia: University of South Carolina Press, 2012.

Lounsbury, J., Fisher, L., Levy, J., and Welsh, D. "An Investigation of Character Strengths in Relation to the Academic Success of College Students." *Individual Differences Research,* 2009, *7*(1), 52–69.

Pearson, P. H. "Relationships Between Global and Specified Measures of Novelty Seeking." *Journal of Clinical and Consulting Psychology,* 1970, *34*(2), 199–204.

Pintrich, P. R., and Schunk, D. H. *Motivation in Education: Theory, Research, and Applications* (2nd ed.). Upper Saddle River, NJ: Merrill, 2002.

Ryan, R., and Deci, E. "Self-Determination Theory and the Facilitation of Intrinsic Motivation, Social Development, and Well-Being." *American Psychologist,* 2000, *55,* 68–78.

Silvia, P. J. *Exploring the Psychology of Interest.* New York: Oxford University Press, 2006.

Silvia, P.J. "Appraisal Components and Emotion Traits: Examining the Appraisal Basis of Trait Curiosity." *Cognition and Emotion,* 2008, *22*(1), 94–114.

Tsai, Y. M., and others. "What Makes Lessons Interesting? The Role of Situational and Individual Factors in Three School Subjects." *Journal of Educational Psychology,* 2008, *100,* 460–472.

EILEEN HULME *is the executive director of the Noel Academy for Strengths-Based Leadership and Education and a professor in the Department of Doctoral Higher Education at Azusa Pacific University.*

DANIEL T. GREEN *is the director of the Master of Entertainment Industry Management program at Carnegie Mellon University. He is currently pursuing his PhD in higher education and organizational leadership at Azusa Pacific University.*

KIMBERLY S. LADD *is director of Career Development and assistant professor of business at Palm Beach Atlantic University.*

NEW DIRECTIONS FOR STUDENT SERVICES • DOI: 10.1002/ss

6

This chapter challenges the contemporary narrative that suggests higher education and student learning are in decline. Prescriptions for strengthening pedagogical processes by adapting principles from appreciative inquiry are also discussed.

Appreciative Inquiry in Teaching and Learning

Laura M. Harrison, Shah Hasan

While K–12 education routinely receives negative press through reporting on issues ranging from low test scores to violence to criticisms of teachers' unions, reproach of higher education is a more recent phenomenon (Hersh and Merrow, 2005). Colleges and universities are still largely seen as places that add value to society through teaching and research, but public support has declined over the past several years (Wheeler and James, 2012). The reasons are complicated and beyond the context of higher education exclusively as most public institutions have faced eroding support in the current era of privatization. An analysis of the decrease in public support for higher education is beyond the scope of this chapter; however, we begin with this point to call attention to the urgency of getting ahead of the curve in how higher education is portrayed. Negatively biased depictions of college life contribute to consequences ranging from declining public investment in higher education to decreased morale for those who work in university settings (Kezar, 2005). One alternative might be to draw attention instead to positively deviant experiences in higher education.

We draw attention to this trend toward negativity in representations of higher education as context for why an appreciative inquiry (AI) perspective is perhaps more urgent in the current zeitgeist. Much of the discourse about college students characterizes them as unfocused, obsessed with iPhones, and overindulged by helicopter parents (Endres and Tisinger, 2007; Ludden, 2012; Taylor, 2006). The dominant narrative about those who teach them paints a similarly bleak picture of educators as disinterested, unavailable, and unable to reach students, particularly the eighteen- to twenty-two-year-old creature that our culture mythologizes. For example, consider this passage from *We're Losing Our Minds: Rethinking*

New Directions for Student Services, no. 143, Fall 2013 © Wiley Periodicals, Inc.
Published online in Wiley Online Library (wileyonlinelibrary.com) • DOI: 10.1002/ss.20061

American Higher Education, part of a prolific genre of works where negative portrayals of students and faculty provide a common theme:

> ... [I]nstruction is mostly lecture-driven and learning, to the extent that it occurs, is mostly a passive, receptive enterprise. In other words, students should come to class, listen carefully, take good notes, and be grateful. Expectations and standards of excellence for students are too often quite low; meeting them requires minimal student (and faculty) effort. (Keeling and Hersh, 2012, p. 20)

Negative, sweeping statements like this increasingly shape the story that is told about college and university life. Given the disconcerting finding of reports highlighting higher education's shortcomings (for example, Association of American Colleges and Universities, 2010; Immerwahr, Johnson, Ott, and Rochkind, 2010; U.S. Department of Education, 2006), ample evidence exists to warrant concern about the quality of student learning on American college campuses. We do not seek to minimize the valid fears, but we worry the discourse has become so negatively skewed that we are in danger of creating a self-fulfilling prophesy about student learning.

There are many valid points about the need for higher education reform. Focusing exclusively on the negative, however, does not inspire change. Heath and Heath (2010) advocate shifting institutional attention from what is wrong in an organization to a deeper analysis of what they call "bright spots." Bright spots refer to those areas in an organization or system that *are* working, which is the heart of AI. In this chapter, we hope to demonstrate the possibilities that can result from a seemingly simple shift from a negative discourse to an AI lens on the issue of student learning.

Having spent most of my (Laura) adult life living and working on college campuses, I have ample opportunities to choose whether to examine student phenomena from either a deficit or an appreciative perspective. For example, consider the love affair students seem to have with technology as they walk, talk, and show up in class glued to their gadgets. A student recently showed me his gloves that come with a built-in device allowing him to text unencumbered while keeping his hands warm. I found this curious, but it did not make me panic about today's youth. I did not go out and buy a pair of these special gloves, but he graciously let me try on his, which led to a great conversation about whether texting helps or hinders our ability to communicate in the twenty-first century. While it is fashionable to criticize young people for their apparent failure to express themselves, Lunsford (2007) found contradictory evidence about the effects of texting, Facebook, and Twitter on student writing. As I walked across campus with the student and his high-tech gloves, I talked to him about this research and he talked to me about how he enjoys texting because it gives him a minute to think through what he really wants to say, especially in heated situations. These kinds of exchanges between teenage students and middle-aged professors happen all the time on college campuses, yet the dominant discourse often fails to capture these interactions in its portrayal of students and educators.

The picture that critics paint of students and educators matters because language creates reality (Greenfield and Ribbins, 1993). When students and educators are bombarded with incomplete, negatively slanted representations of themselves, they internalize them. For example, consider confirmation bias. If one's mental model of eighteen- to twenty-two-year-olds is that they are selfish and privileged, it is very easy for the mind to dismiss counterexamples as outliers. As a result, one starts to see only the selfish and privileged young people and the others become largely invisible. It does not matter how smart or sensitive a person is; this is simply how the mind works (Kahneman, 2011). We see what we are primed to see, and in the case of higher education right now, we are not primed to see the good. Fortunately, AI exists as a tool for recalibrating the lenses through which we experience a phenomenon. By helping leaders access the positive in their organizations, AI creates opportunities for future change built on past and present strengths. In this chapter, we will demonstrate how the premises of AI can be applied to the practice of teaching, and offer examples of what curricular and co-curricular approaches designed from an AI framework can look like.

Appreciative Inquiry

AI is most of all an approach to change that is about intentionally selecting how we frame the reality around us (Whitney and Trosten-Bloom, 2003). How and what we choose to attend to constructs our reality, and the act of inquiry—how we frame and ask our questions—can change us and advance the transformation we seek. In the process of AI, we choose to ask about what works, what is best, and what inspires us, and we use this discerned "positive core" of the past to discover, dream, and design the future destiny we seek to create.

AI is a dialogic cyclical process that engages change actors in defining the change. It begins with a process of discovering and appreciating what is the positive core of the current experience and then using this information to imagine possibilities, and then to design how to achieve and create the desired future (Hammond, 1998). This contrasts with our more conventional heuristic for sorting through our problems: Assess what is, decide what ought to be, and then work to close the *is ought* gap. In the AI process of collectively seeking the positive core and thinking together about how to continue and extend the positive core, change is enacted. Some of our most meaningful experiences in organizational change have come from facilitating a process for people to enact change through AI. I have watched people in the workplace struggle mightily with this way of viewing change; it is, after all, counterintuitive to how we think through managing problems and facilitating change in the workplace.

The chapter by Bloom and colleagues' in this monograph takes a broad lens, using AI as a framework for considering student affairs work. Fifolt and Lander's chapter in this monograph focused on how AI can be applied to organizational improvement. We use the same fundamental principles to examine teaching the application of this powerful approach to teaching and learning.

Appreciative Inquiry in the Classroom

Traditional classrooms can be combative spaces. Professors and students alike carry expectations that inhibit the full range of intellectual expression and expansion. From the ways classrooms tend to be designed to who stands or sits where to the stifled scenes in which we evaluate each other, students and professors often begin their time together from a place of opposition. As a result, students and faculty sometimes approach class defensively, playing prescriptive roles as grade earners or material deliverers rather than expanding the endless possibilities both roles in alternative scenes can offer, particularly when the student-teacher binary is challenged. Fortunately, AI can offer a framework for disrupting these patterns while covering the material, maintaining some semblance of order, and accomplishing the course goals.

The first scene AI can offer is an alternative paradigm for creating more positive learning experiences with respect to how faculty approach the teaching enterprise. Bain (2004) conducted an extensive study of college faculty, examining the practices of sixty-plus professors who had been identified as excellent teachers according to a complex rubric that included both student learning outcomes and colleague feedback among other factors. While Bain (2004) never uses the words *appreciative inquiry,* the six major thematic findings in his study reflect aspects of this theory. For example, one of his major results was that excellent teachers began class with higher expectations than most professors. They operated from the assumption that students were smart and capable of being active participants in their own learning rather than passive recipients of knowledge. As a result, this provided an example of positive "self-fulfilling prophecy—a phenomenon where one's beliefs about the situation not only reflected, but created the reality that was possible (Thatchenkery and Chowdhry, 2007). This distinction is subtle but important. In a similar vein, Kegan and Lahey (2001) theorized speech as generative, emphasizing that the way we talk about a situation not only reflects past experience, but future potential as well. Viewed in the context of the aforementioned negative narratives about students, Bain's (2004) findings articulate important connections between attitude, expectations, and quality of teaching.

NEW DIRECTIONS FOR STUDENT SERVICES • DOI: 10.1002/ss

High expectations alone do not translate into quality learning environments for students. High expectations increase the likelihood that faculty will encourage active participation rather than passive learning, but it takes more than wishful thinking to translate this good intention into action. Part of why active learning contains a theory-practice gap involves what Wiggins and McTighe (2005) called the *expert blindspot*. I (Laura) used to feel frustrated when I thought I was offering students the freedom and flexibility to take ownership of an assignment by not providing stringent guidelines, only to receive work that did not reflect my expectations of student performance. Now I realize the paradigm under which I was operating contained elements of the expert blindspot. The expert blindspot phenomenon explains why it is generally difficult for anyone over the age of thirty to teach a sixteen-year-old how to drive a car, for example. The thirty-plus-year-old takes things like putting your foot on the brake and starting the car for granted, having done them so many times that they become defaults that do not need to be set every time they drive. Teenagers, however, need to be told these basic facts before they can understand how to put the car in reverse, back up, shift to drive, and so forth. The same principle operates in classrooms every day. If professors give a group assignment, for instance, they tend to assume students learned somewhere along the way how to engage as a team. The reality, however, is often different. Students have probably completed group projects in the past, but there is a good chance that no one ever explained to them what to do if they got stuck, how to confront a person not pulling his or her own weight, how to confront a controlling personality, and all of the other intricacies that characterize what it means to be part of a functional team. Without this foundational knowledge, students' performance may suffer not because they lowered their commitment to an assignment, but because they actually lacked the necessary tools to complete it.

The expert blindspot provides a powerful example of how an AI lens makes a difference in diagnosing classroom challenges. It would be easy to interpret students' low performance on an assignment as evidence that they either lack intelligence or motivation, engaging in the aforementioned practice of confirmation bias. An appreciative lens expands the possible choices, allowing for alternative interpretations based on the assumption that students want to learn. In response, faculty can empower students with the tools they need to be successful rather than engaging a defeatist attitude about their own or their students' challenges in the classroom.

Professors can begin with high expectations and take all the right steps to empower active learning only to undermine these efforts by engaging in traditional grading practices. Like education itself, grading appears as an objective practice unbound by ideological choices. One typical default that often occurs with grading is that we operate from a competitive, scarcity mentality without even realizing it. There are a certain (mostly arbitrary) number of A's that we will give, and those will be distributed depending how students perform in comparison with one another. Zander and Zander (2000) describe how they shifted this conventional approach toward an appreciative perspective, allowing students in their classes to start with an A. They required students to submit a letter written in the past tense about what they did to earn that A, being as explicit as possible about what made their performance so stellar. This allowed students to move from a competitive focus on peers to a deeper understanding of how to draw out their own highest potential. They took more risks and obsessed less about failure when professors evaluated them from an appreciative perspective.

Another problematic default that occurs in traditional grading is the focus on past rather than future performance. Educators often employ summative grading practices like final exams and end-of-term papers as evidence for measuring what students learned throughout a course. While there is nothing inherently wrong with these indicators, we tend to treat them as defaults rather than examining what we hope to achieve at a deeper level through grading. By using methods that focus on the past, we unwittingly set students up for a zero-sum game. Either they learned the material or they did not. Formative grading practices offer an alternative by simply shifting the focus from grading on students' past performance to their future potential. Examples of formative assessment include allowing students to turn in drafts of papers and portfolios that can be revised and resubmitted throughout a term as the students' thinking grows and deepens. Treating students and their work as works in progress rather than done deals reflects an appreciative paradigm about what they might accomplish in the future.

These shifts toward an appreciative paradigm are subtle but powerful. In addition to helping us create less stagnant, more generative learning environments for students, they provide some benefits to educators as well. For example, formative grading helped me realize that summative course evaluations made little sense when I received feedback long after the completion of the course. So I started asking students for ongoing feedback while the class was still in session, allowing me to treat myself as a work in progress in much the same way I approached my students. This took the pressure off, allowed me to be more creative, and built credibility among my students who could see my commitment to continual self-improvement operationalized. A common criticism of AI is that it's unrealistically optimistic, that it fails to account for real challenges by simply whitewashing them with positivity. Barbara Ehrenreich's (2010) book, *Brightsided: How Positive Thinking Is Undermining America*, provides a compelling example of this argument. Similarly, students sometimes struggle with the autonomy that comes with appreciative approaches, having grown accustomed to teacher-centered pedagogies that allow them more anonymity and passivity (Cockell and McAuthur-Blair, 2012). We acknowledge these valid critiques and offer the previous points not as a panacea for the legitimate challenges of teaching, but as ways of expanding the possible approaches. Conventional practices like lectures and final exams have value; an appreciative paradigm simply enlarges the possibilities, particularly when educators find themselves stuck and needing a different path.

Appreciative Inquiry Beyond the Classroom

Much of what students learn emerges from outside the classroom. In their friendships and relationships and in their spheres of community (peer student groups, clubs, and organizations, and in more residential settings, sororities, and residence hall neighborhoods), students learn from each other and faculty and staff mentors, ways of being, knowing and acting in their world through their collective projects. Progressing from tentative imitation to more considered choices, students experience from their work of organizing and planning activities, a social and intellectual enculturation that they carry forward after graduation. Strongly pronounced campus cultural norms and the guidance and facilitation of student development professionals hopefully and intentionally shape the physical and social collegial environment to create opportunities for students to learn. Campus employment and voluntary positional roles are invested with learning outcomes. Increasingly, opportunities for service learning and joining efforts to act to serve others in need combined with reflection and other contemplative activities are aimed to facilitate for students the clarifying of values and advancement to the next "higher" level of perspective (Kegan, 1982, 1998), intellectual and social development (Chickering and Reisser, 1993; Perry, 1998), and moral reasoning (Gilligan, 1993; Kohlberg, 1984).

AI can be utilized deliberately in shaping experiences and processes designed to focus student attention and reflection on both the dynamic complexity of their world and the agency of purpose available to them. Reflecting on dynamic complexity would help students appreciate the interrelationships of phenomena, that in a world where resources easily travel between global markets, buying a T-shirt at the bookstore is related to the subsistence of labor in places far away. Agency of purpose then permits the claiming and clarifying of intentional effort in the context of our values. The realization that an act of selecting which T-shirts to buy or not buy affords an opportunity for agency—to act in consonance with developing values. Choices and activities both inside and outside the classroom present options for how we frame learning and inquiry.

AI is experienced often as counterintuitive to our conventional gestures for solving problems. We raise and educate our children to focus on closing the gap between aspiration and actuality. We encourage the learning and discernment that allows them to identify and understand achievement gaps and then to sort through and fix what is wrong so that we can close the gap. AI gives us an opportunity to design learning experiences for students to think through a challenge utilizing a model for making change through a disruptive alternative process that yields its own learning. Jean Baker Miller's (1986) research on women, summarized in what she called Relational Culture Theory suggested that women (and men) grow and learn through their relationships and conversation with others (Miller and Stiver, 1997). Outside the classroom, AI can provide projects of inquiry and learning replete with pedagogical potential to generate agency and growth.

AI functions essentially as a reframing of inquiry on matters of significance. AI would frame the question of student retention not as "Why are students leaving?" but rather "Why are students staying?" And this question would be asked not to students who are leaving but to students who have stayed and would love to stay. In the example of students planning and organizing an activity, AI would frame the preparatory inquiry ("How do we get more people to be enthusiastic and participate?") that precedes organizing the activity in a project that engages student organizers to fan out and ask prospective participants to imagine and vividly describe the best possible activity ("the positive core"). The campus activity could then be designed around the summary elements of the identified positive core. Perhaps even more importantly, the action of inquiry itself creates, for all who asked and answered about the positive core, the desired change (enthusiastic participation). This is called the *Poetic Principle of Appreciative Inquiry* (Whitney and Trosten-Bloom, 2003).

Beyond successful execution, framing work and effort in terms of AI, provides the additional benefits of reinforcing the beliefs and experiences that lead to an upward self-efficacy spiral of "one's capabilities to organize and execute the courses of action required to produce given attainments" (Bandura, 1977, p. 193). Ascertaining and attending to the positive past and using it to chart the future builds confidence. Among other benefits, these learning activities are aspirational rehearsals for work and life, because ample evidence exists that repeated iterations of successful framing, planning, and executing projects together are correlated to confidence (Bendoly, Thomas, and Capra, 2010). The application of AI in programmed learning activities outside of the classroom can be a powerful source of growth and development.

Conclusion

In this chapter, we have focused primarily on applying appreciative inquiry principles to curricular and co-curricular learning. As we know, learning does not occur in a vacuum; the culture of the institution where the learning takes place plays a critical role in determining whether a deficit or AI paradigm will prevail. While individuals can make choices within their sphere of influence, the institutional context can enhance or inhibit an AI perspective. Ideally, individual efforts to bring an AI lens to a learning environment are coupled with organizational commitment to use AI to inform decision making and policy development at the systemic level. When individuals and organizations commit to an AI framework, the possibilities for seamlessness in both student learning and the administration that supports this learning are enhanced.

The time is ripe for applying AI beyond individual and single-institutional contexts. On the macro level of the higher education system, AI has the potential to help us change course from the unfortunate direction in which we fear we're headed. The dominant discourse about colleges and universities is heavily skewed toward the negative. While it may be tempting to ignore these criticisms as mere annoyances, we must remember that language both reflects and creates reality. Critics play an important role in keeping institutions honest; the options are not exclusively writing them off or internalizing their perspective. An alternative path is to implement AI itself to look at the parts of the message that might be the most useful and refrain from obsessing about the less helpful aspects.

An aspect of the criticism we find useful is the narrative about mission creep. Many scholars believe higher education has lost its way, particularly with regard to its original purpose as a public good designed to prepare citizens for the responsibility of democracy (McLaren, 2003; Nussbaum, 2010; Washburn, 2005). Reinvigorating the notion of higher education as any kind of good—public or otherwise—presents a key function of any attempt to enact a changed portrayal our nation's colleges and universities.

In the past, the public supported higher education generously, understanding colleges and universities as part of a proverbial tide that lifted all boats. When the dominant cultural narrative of higher education shifted from public good to private capital, taxpayer support declined (Hersh and Merrow, 2005). Understandably, if the public perceives higher education as a tool to enhance one's personal human capital, why would it want to pay for someone else's participation? Eroding public support for higher education, coupled with a dampened economy more generally, adds to the systemic challenges facing this important institution. How does higher education begin to engage the change that is called for in the face of these retracted resources and support? How does higher education begin to refocus its commitment to the initial ideals of public education for the greater good? We believe the answers to these questions lie in using the tools of AI to inform the learning that takes place within the curriculum and co-curriculum, administrative support, and discourse in which we all engage as professionals working in higher education institutions. AI can play an important role in solving the mission creep that has led to declining support for higher education. By identifying, building on, and telling the story of the ways in which higher education positively impacts the lives of students and changes the roles of student and teacher in revised scenes of potential, we have the potential to add balance to the discourse and build momentum for increased support of this vital institution.

References

Association of American Colleges and Universities. *Raising the Bar: Employers' Views on College Learning in the Wake of the Economic Downturn.* Washington, D.C.: National Center for Public Policy and Higher Education and Public Agenda, 2010.

Bain, K. *What the Best College Teachers Do.* Cambridge, Mass.: Harvard University Press, 2004.

Bandura, A. "Self-Efficacy: Toward a Unifying Theory of Behavior Change." *Psychological Review*, 1977, *84*, pp. 191–215.

Bendoly, E., Thomas, D., and Capra, C. "Multilevel Social Dynamics Considerations for Project Management Decision Makers: Antecedents and Implications of Group Member Tie Development." *Decision Sciences*, 2010, *41*(3), 459–490.

Chickering, A., and Reisser, L. *Education and Identity.* San Francisco: Jossey-Bass, 1993.

Cockell, J., and McArthur-Blair, J. (2012). *Appreciative Inquiry in Higher Education: A Transformative Force/Jeanie Cockell, Joan McArthur-Blair* San Francisco: Jossey-Bass 2012.

Ehrenreich, B. *Bright-Sided: How Positive Thinking Is Undermining America* (1st Picador ed.). New York: Picador, 2010.

Endres, J., and Tisinger, D. "Digital Distractions: College Students in the 21st Century." 2007. Retrieved from http://www.nacada.ksu.edu/Clearinghouse/AdvisingIssues/Digital-Distractions.htm

Gilligan, C. *In a Different Voice: Psychological Theory and Women's Development.* Cambridge, Mass.: Harvard University Press, 1993.

Greenfield, T., and Ribbins, P. (eds.). *Greenfield on Educational Administration: Towards a Humane Science.* New York: Routledge, 1993.

Hammond, S. *The Thin Book of Appreciative Inquiry.* Plano, TX: Thin Book, 1998.

Heath, C., and Heath, D. *Switch: How to Change Things When Change Is Hard.* New York: Broadway Books Random House, 2010.

Hersh, R., and Merrow, J. *Declining by Degrees: Higher Education at Risk.* New York: Palgrave Macmillan, 2005.

Immerwahr, J., Johnson, J., Ott, A., and Rochkind, J. *Squeeze Play 2010: Continued Public Anxiety on Cost, Harsher Judgments on How Colleges Are Run.* Washington, D.C.: National Center of Public Policy and Higher Education and Public Agenda, 2010.

Kahneman, D. *Thinking, Fast and Slow.* New York: Farrar, Straus, and Giroux, 2011.

Keeling, R., and Hersh, R. *We're Losing Our Minds: Rethinking American Higher Education.* New York: Palgrave Macmillan, 2012.

Kegan, R. *The Evolving Self: Problem and Process in Human Development.* Cambridge, Mass.: Harvard University Press, 1982.

Kegan, R. *In Over Our Heads: The Mental Demands of Modern Life.* Cambridge, Mass.: Harvard University Press, 1998.

Kegan, R., and Lahey, L. L. *How the Way We Talk Can Change the Way We Work: Seven Languages for Transformation* (1st ed.). San Francisco: Jossey-Bass, 2001.

Kezar, A. J. "Creating a Megamovement: A Vision Toward Regaining the Public Social Charter." In A. J. Kezar, A. C. Chambers, and J. Burkhardt (eds), *Higher Education for the Public Good: Emerging Voices from a National Movement.* San Francisco: Jossey-Bass, 2005.

Kohlberg, L. *The Psychology of Moral Development: The Nature and Validity of Moral Stages.* New York: Harper and Row, 1984.

Ludden, J. "Helicopter Parents Hover in the Workplace." 2012. http://www.npr.org/2012/02/06/146464665/helicopter-parents-hover-in-the-workplace?sc=fbandcc=fp

Lunsford, A. "Our Semi-literate Youth? Not So Fast." 2007. http://www.stanford.edu/group/ssw/cgi-bin/materials/OPED_Our_Semi-Literate_Youth.pdf

McLaren, P. "Revolutionary Pedagogy in Post-Revolutionary Times." In A. Darder, M. Baltodano, and R. Torres (eds.), *The Critical Pedagogy Reader* (pp. 151–184). New York: Routledge Falmer, 2003.

Miller, J. B. *Toward a New Psychology of Women* (2nd ed.). Boston: Beacon Press, 1986.

Miller, J. B., and Stiver, I. P. *The Healing Connection: How Women Form Relationships in Therapy and in Life.* Boston: Beacon Press, 1997.

Nussbaum, M. *Not for Profit: Why Democracy Needs the Humanities.* Princeton, NJ: Princeton University Press, 2010.

Perry, W. G. *Forms of Intellectual Development in the College Years: A Scheme.* San Francisco: Jossey-Bass, 1998.

Taylor, M. "Generation NeXt Comes to College: 2006 Updates and Emerging Issues." *A Collection of Papers on Self-Study and Institutional Improvement,* 2006, 2(2), 48–55.

Thatchenkery, T., and Chowdhry, D. (2007). *Appreciative Inquiry and Knowledge Management: A Social Constructivist Perspective.* Northhampton, Mass.: Edward Elgar.

U.S. Department of Education. *A Test of Leadership: Charting the Future of U.S. Higher Education.* Washington, D.C.: Commission appointed by Secretary of Education Margaret Spellings, 2006.

Washburn, J. *University Inc.: The Corporate Corruption of Higher Education.* New York: Basic Books, 2005.

Wheeler, B., and James L. "The Marketecture of Community." *Educause Review,* 2012, 47(6), 66.

Whitney, D., and Trosten-Bloom, A. *The Power of Appreciative Inquiry: A Practical Guide to Positive Change.* San Francisco: Berrett-Koehler, 2003.

Wiggins, G., and McTighe, J. *Understanding by Design.* Alexandria, Vir.: Association for Supervision and Curriculum Development, 2005.

Zander, R., and Zander, B. *The Art of Possibility: Transforming Professional and Personal Life.* Cambridge, Mass.: Harvard Business School Press, 2000.

LAURA M. HARRISON is an assistant professor in Higher Education and Student Affairs at Ohio University.

SHAH HASAN is dean of the College of Business at Urbana University.

7

Social justice and community service have strong traditions in higher education. In this chapter, the authors describe ways in which positive psychology and appreciative inquiry inform the pursuit of social justice through community service activities.

Promoting Social Justice Through Appreciative Community Service

Peter C. Mather, Erin Konkle

Much of the positive psychology scholarship to date has focused on enhancing our understanding of how to achieve a sense of well-being, but considerably less guidance exists on how to disseminate well-being (Thin, 2011). In addition, little research and writing on positive psychology has focused on translating the wealth of positive psychology research to populations in high-poverty communities.

While positive psychology has not, in large part, attended to people in poverty, there is a growing body of literature attending to these concerns (Diener and Oishi, 2000; Linley, Bhaduri, Sen Sharma, and Govindji, 2011; Schwartz and Melech, 2000). Because of positive psychology's focus on enriching lives, and due to higher education's interest in dealing with injustice and inequality (Johnson and O'Grady, 2006; Osei-Kofi, Shahjahan, and Patton, 2010), it is appropriate to consider ways in which positive psychology principles can be applied to higher education's efforts to improve conditions for historically oppressed individuals and communities.

Higher education's work with oppressed groups is generally framed as social justice. Social justice is directed toward "bringing about a more equitable distribution of society's wealth" (Hoppe, 2004, p. 139). Social justice approaches to community service and service-learning aim to awaken participants to injustice and to catalyze action (Exley, 2004, p. 87). These community service activities are wide ranging, from gaining exposure to injustice by performing service work in high-poverty communities to engaging in political protests.

In this chapter, we present an appreciative orientation approach to promoting social justice in high-poverty communities: The appreciative framework of community service is informed by emerging scholarship from

New Directions for Student Services, no. 143, Fall 2013 © Wiley Periodicals, Inc.
Published online in Wiley Online Library (wileyonlinelibrary.com) • DOI: 10.1002/ss.20062

positive psychology and appreciative inquiry (AI), and both models have shown evidence of success in improving the quality of life in high-poverty communities (Biswas-Diener and Patterson, 2011; Gawande, 2008; Kretzmann and McKnight, 2003; Linley and others, 2011).

It should be noted that some of the prominent positive psychology findings pertinent to community service corresponds more directly to a *charity* approach than to social justice. Consonant with the charity approach, there is considerable positive psychology research that focuses on bolstering personal fulfillment and happiness through performing acts of kindness (Lyubomirsky, 2008). Lyubomirsky's considerable research on charitable behavior confirms the positive influence that engaging in service activities—including even the simplest of gestures—has on the giver's well-being.

While positive psychology research informs the charity models of service, there is also a growing body of social justice–oriented research focused on improving lives of oppressed and marginalized persons and communities (Biswas-Diener and Patterson, 2011; Linley, Bhaduri, Sen Sharma, and Govindji, 2011; and Thin, 2011). One of the primary appreciative models of practice is asset-based community development (ABCD) (Kretzmann and McKnight, 2003). The asset-based model emphasizes identifying, nurturing, and capitalizing on individual and collective strengths that exist within poor communities. According to Kretzmann and McKnight, meaningful and significant community development only occurs when the community itself is invested in the effort. This stands in contrast to the charity model, which emphasizes help from outside agents over action from community members.

While the appreciative framework resonates with social justice's focus on structural barriers to equity, it offers a unique lens on poverty-related problems. For instance, Thin (2011) has argued that positive psychology may influence considerations of the meanings and sources of "justice," moving people to consider justice as "being about the distribution and sharing of *well-being*, not only about access to resources" (p. 47). This orientation is supported by research findings suggesting that economic realities are often overemphasized and matters such as family and health are underemphasized in considerations of well-being (Graham, 2009). Thus, while economic realities are not ignored in asset-based models, the appreciative framework gives them less emphasis than do dominant social justice models. Diener and Diener (2011) recommend psychosocial prosperity as a development goal; prosperity in this vein includes social characteristics such as supportive social relationships, competence and mastery, and subjective well-being.

Both social justice and appreciative community frameworks are based on the notion that effective and positive changes require fundamental, systemic adjustments at both a cultural and an individual level. Thin (2011) points out that numerous social pathologies stand in the way of living a full life. Materialism is certainly among the barriers to well-being, as are oppressive phenomena such as sexism and racism. These barriers to well-being are evident in communities ranging from upper economic class to high poverty, and each type of community has much to learn from the other.

While cultural barriers to well-being are evident, seldom will effective change occur through direct confrontation of these pathologies, especially from outsiders (Thin, 2011). Thus, appreciative development approaches often emphasize change *within* individuals and communities. According to Thin, positive psychology approaches generally center on engaging communities positively, and using the emerging wholeness of people to lead to systemic change.

In addition to the practical barriers associated with attempting to create change by direct confrontation, there are also philosophical and ethical arguments against such approaches. Block (2008) points out that dissent and rebellion, common features of the social justice paradigm are sometimes antithetical to meaningful change. He states:

> On the surface, rebellion claims to be against monarchy, dominion, or oppression. Too often it turns out to be a vote for monarchy, dominion, or patriarchy. Rebellion is most often not a call for transformation or a new context, but simply a complaint that others control the monarchy and not us. … Any time we act in reaction, even to evil, we are giving power to what we are in reaction to. … The real problem with rebellion is that it is such fun. It avoids taking responsibility, operates on the high ground, is fueled by righteousness, gives legitimacy to blame, and is a delightful escape from the unbearable burden of being accountable. (p. 134)

An appreciative approach entails taking responsibility for change rather than relinquishing power to outside parties. Resting the power for change within the community is indicative of a belief in the strengths and assets of poor communities. Focusing on assets possessed by the community allays the complications resulting from overdependence on outside benefactors.

In this chapter, we present two community service practices that were developed out of an appreciative framework. Both of these approaches focus on leveraging the strengths that exist within communities in order to foster a more just society. The first approach, asset mapping, is closely aligned with positive psychology's strengths movement. The second model presented is based on an adaptation of AI's 4-D model of institutional improvement (Bloom, Hutson, and He, 2008).

Asset Mapping

> Every single person has capacities, abilities and gifts. Living a good life depends on whether those capacities can be used, abilities expressed and gifts given. If they are, the person will be valued, feel powerful and

well-connected to the people around them. And the community around the person will be more powerful because of the contribution the person is making. (Kretzmann and McKnight, 2003, p. 13)

The practice of asset mapping begins with identifying the community's and community members' strengths. There is a plethora of research attesting to the benefits derived from focusing on strengths for both organizations and individuals (Govindji and Linley, 2007; Harter, Schmidt, and Hayes, 2002; Seligman, Steen, Park, and Peterson, 2005). Linley and colleagues (2011) described a strengths-based initiative in a slum community in India. The conditions of this community were described in stark terms, for example, one toilet serving 2,500 people; homes are made of patched together materials such as billboard remnants, corrugated iron, concrete pipes, and so on; and floors are made compacted dirt. Despite these difficult material conditions, the researchers described strong social connections among the community members, as demonstrated through strong conversational behaviors, children finding happiness through play, and so on.

In order to uncover the strengths in this seemingly desperate community, Linley and colleagues (2011) conducted interpreter-mediated interviews designed to identify community members' strengths. Interviewers attempted to elicit the naming of strengths by asking about daily and periodic activities, with a focus on what activities participants enjoyed doing and what it was about the activities they enjoyed. They also asked about visions for the future, what they do best, what they would like to do but do not have the opportunity, and who in the community supports and encourages them. These interviews led to the development of interest groups, such as a sewing club that served as a collective, bonding activity, and a source of income.

In inner-city Indianapolis, Broadway United Methodist Church conducts strengths interviews with members of the community, and has found through this process that interviews are most productive when people are asked about their neighbors' and family members' strengths rather than their own (Mike Mather, personal communication, April 11, 2013). They have found this approach to be more effective that soliciting strengths directly from individuals due to the reality that individuals often do not recognize their own strengths (Linley, 2008).

Another effective asset-based strategy, a supplement to strengths interviews, involves the telling of community stories. Block (2008) and McKnight and Block (2012) provided guidance for soliciting stories that are restorative. They assert that it is important to encourage stories about "talents, properties, and gifts" (McKnight and Block, 2012, p. 95), rather than about deficiencies.

Students involved in community service programs can solicit these stories by asking general questions about community strengths or questions based on specific observations:

- "Tell me the story of how this community center came to be."
- "I notice there is a lot of laughter when people get together; tell me about what coming together means to you."
- "What goals and dreams do you have for the children of the community?"

Service groups can record stories and present them, along with the results of strength assessments, to the community. Often, community members are not aware of positive features of their community. This was the case in the story told by Mike Mather (2010) about Maya, a member of a high-poverty community in Indianapolis, who tutors young people in reading and writing. Few people in the neighborhood knew of Maya's involvement with these students. Once people became aware of her work, the community embraced her contributions and celebrated them publicly. Recognizing activities performed by Maya and others like her remind people that fundamental assets required to strengthen the communities are already present; members of the community do not need to wait for someone outside to save or fix them.

It is important to keep in mind that assets do not need to have ostensible economic valuable in order to have worth. So assets that may commonly be considered unimportant for community development are, in fact, valued. For instance, Kretzmann and McKnight (2003) refer to the importance of community members' artistic talents for bolstering self-expression and self-esteem, fostering vision and creativity, acknowledging cultural assets, and developing productive personal disciplines. Thus, there are unique and important roles for people's artistic talents in building up communities. Communities can also be enriched by cultivating a host of non-economic relational strengths, such as the ability to listen and the gift of encouraging others. Community well-being relies on strengthening social fabric as much or more than cultivating financial resources or earning potential.

The process of mapping community assets is conducted with material derived from strengths interviews, inventories of community capacities (see Kretzmann and McKnight, 2003), and from community stories. The service group should also collect a list of community associations, businesses, institutions, and other types of environmental resources that are also important assets. Individuals and groups (e.g., youth, artists, seniors, or persons with disabilities) can then be mapped to these potential community partners. As an example, many communities and institutions do not recognize the assets offered by their senior citizens.

Figure 7.1 illustrates potential connections between Maya and other neighborhood resources. For instance, Maya's work can be enhanced by connections to the area library. In return, the library will be enriched by the participation of children who have not been patrons previously. Maya's work directly benefits children, whose engagement with Maya gives her

NEW DIRECTIONS FOR STUDENT SERVICES • DOI: 10.1002/ss

Figure 7.1. Potential Connections between Maya and Other Neighborhood Resources

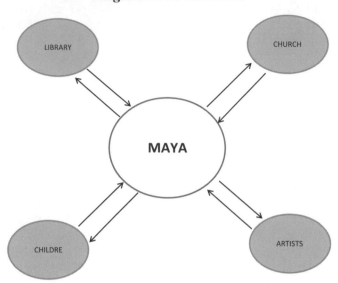

human connections that strengthen her life. The local church provides a venue for celebrating Maya's work, and the church benefits by its connection to the community. Local artists could engage participating children in finding alternative ways of expression, thus contributing to Maya's literacy work, and so on. Maps can also be drawn with groups in the center of the schema, rather than individuals (Kretzmann and McKnight, 2003). Thus, asset maps can be drawn for categories of people, such as community seniors, artists, or people with disabilities. Maps recognize both the realized and unrealized assets the groups bring and the resources that can enrich their lives within the community.

One of the challenges of this type of activity for community service groups is that the formal relationship between the service team and the community is often short-lived due to curricular or other scheduling constraints or due to geographic realities. In regard to short-term community service experiences, it is especially important for service teams from colleges and universities to work closely with a host nongovernmental organization (NGO) or other community partners to see whether there are possibilities for the NGO to continue the asset-based community development work following the departure of the service team. We have found that sharing the asset mapping approach with NGOs and other community partners can shape the organizations' future work with communities.

This asset-based approach can be a stand-alone exercise or part of a larger service project that service groups can conduct in a community. In a service-learning-based program in Ecuador, a class from Ohio University augments the asset identification and mapping activity with other initiatives, including construction work and educational play with children. These activities, when conducted side-by-side with community members, can provide additional opportunities to build relationships with community members and to recognize community strengths.

The following appreciative education model for practice provides a way of conceiving of an overall approach a service team might take with a community. Asset-based community development strategies can be employed within this framework.

Appreciative Education in Service: A Model for Practice

The appreciative advising model (Bloom, Hutson, and He, 2008; Cooperrider and Srivastva, 1987) can serve as a useful framework for planning and implementing community-based service programs that foster positive emotional engagement and well-being. Bloom, Huston, and He expanded Cooperrider's four D's to six cyclical phases—Disarm, Discover, Dream, Design, Deliver, and Don't Settle—that are designed to build on positive experiences and strengths that are manifest in the community.

Appreciative advising is easily adapted to the planning and implementing of community engagement programs, from service abroad trips, to service-learning courses, to short-term programs. Members of the university community as well as community partners important to the development of meaningful and sustainable programs can utilize the six phases.

Disarm. The Disarm stage is about breaking down barriers between students and community members. Setting a positive tone early in the process for all stakeholders sends an inclusive message that every person and his or her contributions are valued. A positive tone also opens up avenues of communication necessary for creating meaningful programs.

In a two-week service-learning program in Honduras (Mather, Given, Hendrickson, and Lash, 2010), the first interaction between community members and the service group is a social mixer, which can include a range of activities, from music performances to friendly competitions such as relay races. These activities reduce barriers (i.e., "disarming") among participants, and establish a solid foundation for building relationships throughout the week.

It can also be "disarming" to begin from the first day to highlight the gifts and assets of community members and recognize that they are no less valued than the assets of the group that are guests in the community. It is important to undermine from the beginning the notion that one group exclusively possesses skills and gifts to be bestowed upon another.

Discover. University and community partners come to the table with diverse needs and previous experiences. Service participants should be prepared to avoid defaulting to easy answers about causes of poverty and related social problems. Participants should be open to learning about the needs and assets of each stakeholder to ensure that the benefits of a program are maximized and to acknowledge the multiple gifts that come together in the community. Understanding each stakeholder's previous experiences and what strengths and assets they bring to the engagement program can make the planning process more effective.

Not all projects or programs are right for every community partner. Spending time listening to and learning about each person's strengths, needs, goals, and prior experiences will provide rich and important information. Focusing particularly on past projects or successes that community partners believed to be successful and meaningful can help to create a foundation to build new projects and create new successes.

In the Honduras program, this important phase is initiated by members of a local NGO working with the community to identify assets and needs prior to the service-learning group's arrival. With the groundwork laid, the service team comes into the village prepared to address this particular community's self-identified needs and priorities. Because the organization has a continuous presence in the area, they are in a strong position to recognize the gifts and needs of the community members.

Also prior to the service group's arrival in the community, students are put into research teams—based on personal and scholarly interests—to gain an in-depth understanding of the lives of community members. Teams have investigated questions about mental health challenges and resources, the experiences of adolescents in the educational system, and community members' assessments of the changes made to their community by the local NGO and service teams. The asset mapping process described above is also a potential investigative exercise.

Through these research experiences, service-learning class members gain a deeper understanding of the lives of the community members. This serves not only to enrich the relationships, but to engender an understanding of the complexity of poverty-related realities. This understanding can also spark curiosity and intellectual engagement, components of a flourishing life, as discussed by Hulme, Green, and Ladd in Chapter Two of this monograph.

Dream. Dream provides an avenue for all stakeholders to consider other options before committing to one particular path for the community. It is important to take the opportunity to allow university and community partners to think from a big-picture perspective about community goals and aspirations without the constraint of time or resources. This may lead to the development of new ideas and richer programs. It is important to record all of the project ideas in the Dream session—even ones that seem to be the most far-fetched—because components of these pie-in-the-sky dreams could be incorporated into the final project design.

As Harrison and Hasan discussed in Chapter Seven of this volume, faculty or staff leaders often have a need to "possess" questions and answers. However, it is necessary not only to remain open to different ideas, but to structure experiences that invite new ones. This can be accomplished by having different groups (i.e., service team and community members) have responsibility for introducing discussion topics and questions. Since the parties are likely to have diverse perspectives on life and the projects at hand, this will almost certainly broaden participants' frames of reference. In addition, taking time to ask thoughtful big-picture questions can uncover and foster shared themes among participants, which supports experiences of bonding among people who, on the surface, are very different.

Design. The Design phase centers on narrowing the big ideas from the Dream session into manageable and realistic programs that maximize the investment and talents of the stakeholders. Piecing together components from multiple ideas to form one co-created project will give all stakeholders a vested interest in the project's success.

Whenever possible, it is important to allow time in the Design phase to rework and refine the project several times in order to develop a sound and meaningful final product. Participants should explore the resources—temporal, financial, human, and so on—that will be needed to successfully implement the project or program.

It can be useful to work through several different paths for achieving the same outcomes to uncover multiple options. It is valuable to spend time on the details; consider contingency plans, if applicable; and plan the project the whole way through. Wheatley and Frieze's (2011) discussion of communities that have transformed themselves through recognizing and applying their assets offers examples of worthwhile designs.

Deliver. Time spent building relationships, communicating needs and expectations, and co-creating a plan in the previous phases should facilitate smooth program implementation. It is important to continue to communicate frequently throughout the duration of the program. In particular, positive feedback will help to motivate participants and reassure community partners that the experience is valuable. Adjustments may need to be made throughout the program, and expectations should be established that changes will be necessary for successful implementation. It is important to encourage all parties to give open, honest, and constructive feedback, so that adjustments can be made immediately if necessary. Alterations in the plans should be clearly communicated to all involved.

Don't Settle. Reflection is integral to community engagement projects, whether considered service-learning or simply community service programs, because it provides university and community partners with the opportunity to internalize the meaning of their work. Internalization through reflection helps to promote a sense of well-being by nurturing mindfulness and movement outside of one's conventional and customary reality.

As the program comes to a close, it is valuable to look forward and think about next steps and future programs. Generally, service-learning programs focus on reflection that occurs either privately or within the confines of the service team. In this approach based on appreciative education, community members are integral partners in the reflection process. Thus, it is important to create forums where reflection can be performed both individually and in a group setting to enable individuals to process their own experiences, as well as providing the opportunity for the community to reflect on the experience from their own cultural perspective.

Even the most successful projects can improve. It is useful to carve out time to reflect on what would have made the program even more successful if it were to be repeated. Recording this information and making it accessible to all stakeholders is recommended for future use.

Using an appreciative approach to planning community engagement programs provides a multidimensional structure that focuses on leveraging the very best of what the university and community already have to offer. By placing university and community partners together with a shared responsibility for creating, planning, and implementing a program, both parties have a natural interest in seeing it succeed. Additionally, the shared responsibility between both groups can eliminate the power dynamic of having one group seen as the expert, fixing the other.

Conclusion

Providing real assistance to high-poverty communities is no easy task. In particular, higher education institutions committed to making a positive difference must navigate complex political, cultural, and psychosocial considerations in the implementation of service programs. We have argued that positive psychology can serve as a useful theoretical foundation for social justice practice due to its focus on improving lives. In this chapter, we offer asset mapping and appreciative education service activities as useful models for guiding effective partnerships in boosting the quality of life in high-poverty communities. While there is a growing body of evidence of the effectiveness of asset-based community practices (Kretzmann and Puntenney, 2010; Puntenney and Zappia, 2013), the appreciative education in service model is offered as an approach that has intuitive appeal but has not yet been empirically tested. In the spirit of positive psychology, which has a strong basis in empirical research, we have offered this approach with recommendations for continued study on its efficacy.

In its relatively short existence, positive psychology has produced substantial guidance for enhancing life quality. There is a great opportunity for supporters of social justice to apply this rich and growing knowledge base to communities and people that operate on the margins.

References

Biswas-Diener, R. and Patterson, L. "Positive Psychology and Poverty." In R. Biswas-Diener (ed.), *Positive Psychology as Social Change* (pp. 125–140). New York: Springer, 2011.

Block, P. *Community: A Structure of Belonging*. San Francisco: Berrett-Koehler, 2008.

Bloom, J. L., Hutson, B. L., and He, Y. *The Appreciative Advising Revolution*. Champaign, Ill.: Stipes, 2008.

Cooperrider, D. L., and Srivastva, S. "Appreciative Inquiry in Organizational Life." *Research in Organizational Change and Development, 1*(1), 129–169, 1987.

Diener, E., and Diener, C. "Monitoring Psychosocial Prosperity for Social Change." In R. Biswas-Diener (ed.), *Positive Psychology as Social Change* (pp. 53–71). New York: Springer, 2011.

Diener, E., and Oishi, S. "Money and Happiness: Income and Subjective Well-Being Across Nations." In E. Diener and E. M. Suh (eds.), *Culture and Subjective Well-Being* (pp. 185–218). Cambridge, Mass.: MIT Press, 2000.

Exley, R. J. "A Critique of the Civic Engagement Model." In B. W. Speck and S. L. Hoppe (eds.), *Service-Learning: History, Theory, and Issues* (pp. 85–97). Westport, Conn.: Praeger, 2004.

Gawande, A. *Better: A Surgeon's Notes on Performance*. New York: Picador, 2008.

Govindji, R., and Linley, P. A. "Strengths Use, Self-Concordance, and Well-Being: Implications for Strengths Coaching and Coaching Psychologists." *International Coaching Psychology Review,* 2007, *2*(2), 143–153.

Graham, C. *Happiness Around the World: The Paradox of Happy Peasants and Miserable Millionaires*. New York: Oxford University Press, 2009.

Harter, J. K., Schmidt, F. L., and Hayes, T. L. "Business-Unit-Level Relationship between Employee Satisfaction, Employee Engagement, and Business Outcomes: A Meta-Analysis." *Journal of Applied Psychology,* 2002, *87,* 268–279.

Hoppe, S. L. "A Synthesis of the Theoretical Stances." In B. W. Speck and S. L. Hoppe (eds.), *Service-Learning: History, Theory, and Issues* (pp. 137–149). Westport, Conn.: Praeger, 2004.

Johnson, B. T., and O'Grady, C. R. "The Spirit of Service: Exploring Faith, Service, and Justice in Higher Education." Bolton, Mass.: Anker, 2006.

Kretzmann, J. P., and McKnight, J. L. *Building Communities from the Inside Out: A Path Toward Finding and Mobilizing a Community's Assets*. Skokie, Ill.: ACTA Publications, 2003.

Kretzmann, J., and Puntenney, D. "Neighborhood Approaches to Asset Mobilization: Building Chicago's West Side." In A. Goetting and G. P. Green (eds.), *Mobilizing Communities: Asset Building as a Community Development Strategy* (pp. 112–129). Philadelphia: Temple University Press, 2010.

Linley, A. *Average to A+: Realising Strengths in Yourself and Others*. Coventry, U.K.: CAPP Press, 2008.

Linley, P. A., Bhaduri, A., Sen Sharma, D., and Govindji, R. "Strengthening Underprivileged Communities: Strengths-Based Approaches as a Force for Social Change in Community Development. In R. Biswas-Diener (ed.), *Positive Psychology as Social Change* (pp. 141–158). New York: Springer, 2011.

Lyubomirsky, S. *The How of Happiness: A Practical Approach to Getting the Life You Want*. New York: Penguin Press, 2008.

Mather, P. C., Given, B., Hendrickson, K., and Lash, A. "Listening to Santa Rita: A Critical Examination of Service-Learning. *Journal of College and Character,* 2010, *11*(3), 1–12. doi: 10.2202/1940-1639.1233

Mather, M. "Have Conversations and Have Faith: Trading 'Us and Them' for 'All of Us.'" In L. A. Goleman (ed.) *Living Our Story: Narrative Leadership and Congregational Culture* (pp. 129–140). Herndon, Vir.: The Alban Institute, 2010.

McKnight, J., and Block, P. *The Abundant Community: Awakening the Power of Families and Neighborhoods*. San Francisco: Berret-Koehler, 2012.

Osei-Kofi, N., Shahjahan, R., and Patton, L. "Centering Social Justice in the Study of Higher Education: The Challenges and Possibilities for Institutional Change." *Equity and Excellence in Education,* 2010, *43,* 326–340.

Puntenney, D., and Zappia, B. "Place-Based Strategies for Improving Health Disparities." In K. Fitzpatrick (ed.), *Poverty and Health in America*. Santa Barbara, CA: Greenwood Press, 2013.

Schwartz, S. H., and Melech, G. National Differences in Micro and Macro Worry: Social, Economic, and Cultural Explanations. In E. Diener and E. M. Suh (eds.), *Culture and Subjective Well-Being* (pp. 219–256). Cambridge, Mass.: MIT Press, 2000.

Seligman, M. E. P., Steen, T. A., Park, N., and Peterson, C. "Positive Psychology Progress: Empirical Validation of Interventions." *American Psychologist,* 2005, *60,* 410–421.

Thin, N. "Socially Responsible Cheermongery: On the Sociocultural Contexts and Levels of Social Happiness Policies." In R. Biswas-Diener (ed.), *Positive Psychology as Social Change* (pp. 33–49). New York: Springer, 2011.

Wheatley, M. J., and Frieze, D. *Walk Out, Walk On: A Learning Journey into Communities Daring to Live the Future Now.* San Francisco: Berrett-Koehler, 2011.

PETER C. MATHER *is an associate professor of Higher Education and Student Affairs and secretary to the board of trustees at Ohio University.*

ERIN KONKLE *is a doctoral student in Organizational Leadership, Policy, and Development at the University of Minnesota.*

New Directions for Student Services • DOI: 10.1002/ss

8

This chapter presents a variety of resources for higher education professionals interested in applying appreciative education principles to their work.

Resources and Readings in Positive Psychology

Peter C. Mather, Eileen Hulme

Since Martin Seligman's admonition to his fellow psychologists over a decade ago to focus on human strengths, substantial research has been conducted and many books and articles published to support the work of educators interested in boosting educational and organizational practice. In this sourcebook, we have only scratched the surface of this exciting new field of inquiry. Readers who recognize the potential for enriching their practice are encouraged to further pursue the ever-growing research findings. One of the strengths of positive psychology is its reliance on strong empirical research. In accordance with this important and basic foundation of positive psychology, higher education practitioners are encouraged to be thoughtful consumers of the field's rich resources. The reading list below highlights several resources that we, the editors of this volume, have found to be particularly enriching to our understanding of this field's potential for practice, and we hope that you also will find these resources to be helpful.

Introductory Texts

This section includes two books by Martin Seligman (2002 and 2011), the founder of Positive Psychology. *Authentic Happiness* is a seminal text in the field, and presents a discussion of Seligman's three prongs of happiness: pleasure, engagement, and meaning. *Flourish* provides an updated version of his theory, re-framed as a theory of well-being. Carr's (2004) text presents core frameworks within the field, with extensive supportive psychological research. Peterson's (2006) *A Primer in Positive Psychology* is a strong introduction to the field, similar to Carr's book, but presented more

NEW DIRECTIONS FOR STUDENT SERVICES, no. 143, Fall 2013 © Wiley Periodicals, Inc.
Published online in Wiley Online Library (wileyonlinelibrary.com) • DOI: 10.1002/ss.20058

informally. Snyder and his colleagues (2011) deliver a comprehensive text-book including practical applications and over 50 case studies from leaders in the field.

Carr, A. *Positive Psychology: The Science of Happiness and Human Strengths*. New York: Brunner-Routledge, 2004.

Peterson, C. *A Primer in Positive Psychology*. New York: Oxford University Press, 2006.

Seligman, M. E. P. *Authentic Happiness: Using the New Positive Psychology to Realize Your Potential for Lasting Fulfillment*. New York: The Free Press, 2002.

Seligman, M. E. P. *Flourish: A Visionary New Understanding of Happiness and Well-being*. New York: The Free Press, 2011.

Snyder, C.R., Lopez, S. and Teramoto, J. *Positive Psychology: The Scientific and Practical Explorations of Human Strengths*. Thousand Oaks, Calif.: Sage, 2011.

Positive Emotional Experience

Fredrickson's (2009) book, *Positivity*, provides a strong introduction to research on positive emotional experience, and includes discussion of the "Broaden and Build" theory, which ties positive emotions to creativity and learning. Emmons (2008) and Lopez (2013) share their expertise on specific positive emotional experiences, gratitude, and hope, respectively. We also include two books by Tal Ben-Shahar (2007 and 2009), who is perhaps best known for his popular introductory course in positive psychology at Harvard. These are short books, which include practical recommendations and exercises that could be helpful in fostering student success.

Fredrickson, B. *Positivity: Top-notch Research Reveals the 3 to 1 Ration that will Change Your Life*. New York: Three Rivers Press, 2009.

Ben-Shahar, T. *Happier: Learn the Secrets to Daily Joy and Lasting Fulfillment*. New York: McGraw-Hill, 2007.

Ben-Shahar, T. *The Pursuit of Perfect: How to Stop Chasing Perfection and Start Living a Richer, Happier Life*. New York: McGraw-Hill, 2009.

Emmons, R. A. *Thanks: How Practicing Gratitude can Make you Happier*. New York: Houghton McMiflin, 2008.

Lopez, S. J. *Making Hope Happen: Create the Life you Want for Yourself and Others*. New York: Atria Books, 2013.

Strengths and Engagement

Strengths assessment, particularly Rath's (2007) *StrengthsFinder 2.0* from the Gallup organization, is widely used on college campuses. We also include a link to Values in Action (VIA), an on-line assessment of character strengths. Peterson and Seligman's (2004) substantial *Handbook of Character Strengths and Values*, using the VIA strengths, is positive psychology's counterpart to the *Diagnostic and Statistical Manual of Mental Disorders* (DSM), describing positive characteristics that are recognized across cultures. We include two volumes on strengths application and assessment by Linley and his colleagues (2008 and 2010), helping those who would like to enhance their understanding of how to improve strengths education.

In addition to strengths, this section includes important texts by Dweck (2006) and Kashdan (2009), related to engagement in learning. Dweck's book describes the benefits of a "growth" or development-oriented mindset, as well as strategies for enhancing one's disposition for learning. The importance and formation of curiosity are described in Kashdan's book.

Dweck, C. *Mindset: The New Psychology of Success*. New York: Random House, 2006.

Kashdan, T. *Curious? Discover the Missing Ingredient to a Fulfilling Life*. New York: HarperCollins, 2009.

Linley, P. A. *Average to A+: Realising Strengths in Yourself and Others*. Coventry, England: CAPP Press, 2008.

Linley, P. A., Willars, J., and Biswas-Diener, R. *The Strengths Book: Be Confident, Be Successful, and Enjoy Better Relationships by Realising the Best of You*. Coventry, England: CAPP Press, 2010.

Peterson, C., and Seligman, M. E. P. *Character Strengths and Virtues: A Handbook and Classification*. New York: Oxford University Press, 2004.

Rath, T. *StrengthsFinder 2.0*. New York: Gallup Press, 2007.

Values in Action Institute on Character. *VIA Survey*. (http://www.viacharacter.org/www/)

Coaching and Activities

There is a growing collection of publications focused on assessments and exercises that could be used with college students and staff. Biswas-Diener's (2007 and 2010) two books on positive psychology coaching contain a variety of tools and principles that can be applied to the college setting. Lyubomirsky's (2008) text, *The How of Happiness*, discusses principles behind improving personal well being. This book also presents several proposed positivity targeted interventions, and provides a rich discussion of the research on their effectiveness. Froh and Parks' (2013) book includes a number of classroom-based interventions and teaching tools to use with college students. Lyubomirsky and Kurtz's (2013) book is designed as a personal workbook, but many of the exercises can be applied either in individual advising or group contexts. In *Thriving in Transitions*, Schreiner and her colleagues (2012) present a research-based understanding of student thriving and demonstrate the concept's application to critical college transitions.

Biswas-Diener, R. *Practicing Positive Psychology Coaching: Assessments, Activities, and Strategies for Success*. Hoboken, NJ: Wiley & Sons, 2010.

Biswas-Diener, R., and Dean, B. *Positive Psychology Coaching: Putting the Science of Happiness to Work for Your Clients*. Hoboken, NJ: Wiley & Sons, 2007.

Froh, J. J., and Parks, A. C. *Activities for Teaching Positive Psychology: A Guide for Instructors*. Washington, D.C.: American Psychological Association, 2013.

Lyubomirsky, S. *The How of Happiness: A Scientific Approach to Getting the Life You Want*. New York: The Penguin Press, 2008.

Lyubomirsky, S., and Kurtz, J. *Positively Happy: Routes to Sustainable Happiness*. Createspace Independent Publishing, 2013.

Schreiner, L., Louis, M., and Nelson, D. *Thriving in Transitions: A Research-Based Approach to College Student Success*. Columbia, SC: The University of South Carolina Press, 2012.

Appreciative Inquiry and Positive Organizations

Appreciative inquiry (AI) is an important tool for organizational improvement. The book by AI pioneers Cooperrider and Whitney (2005) provides a strong introduction with several examples from the corporate world. The book by Cockell, McArthur-Blair, and Schiller (2012) adapts the AI approach to administrative and classroom environments in higher education. Lewis' (2011) book blends positive leadership and appreciative inquiry, providing case studies and examples of effective interventions. Similarly, the edited volume by Linley, Harrington, and Page (2010) draws from a range of disciplines to provide recent thinking on appreciative-based change in organizations. Dutton, Quinn, and Cameron's (2003) edited volume presents concepts related to positive leadership, under the umbrella of positive organizational scholarship (POS). Luthans and his colleagues (2007) introduce the concept of psychological capital (PsyCap) in the context of organizational performance. PsyCap relates to characteristics such as resilience, optimism, and hope, which are also important correlates of student success.

Cockell, J., McArthur-Blair, J., and Schiller, M. *Appreciative Inquiry in Higher Education: A Transformative Force*. San Francisco: Jossey-Bass, 2012.

Cooperrider, D. L., and Whitney, D. *Appreciative Inquiry: A Positive Revolution in Change*. San Francisco: Berrett-Koehler, 2005.

Dutton, J. E., Quinn, R. E., and Cameron, K. (eds.) *Positive Organizational Scholarship: Foundations of a New Discipline*. San Francisco: Berrett-Koehler, 2003.

Lewis, S. *Positive Psychology at Work: How Positive Leadership and Appreciative Inquiry Create Inspiring Organizations*. Chichester, England: Wiley-Blackwell, 2011.

Linley, P. A., Harrington, S., and Page, N. *Oxford Handbook of Positive Psychology and Work*. New York: Oxford University Press, 2010.

Luthans, F., Youseff, C., and Avolio, B. *Psychological Capital: Developing the Human Competitive Edge*. New York: Oxford University Press, 2007

Appreciative Social Justice

Asset-based community development arose separately from positive psychology and appreciative inquiry, but it shares the fundamental principle that positive change occurs when focusing on gifts and assets rather than deficiencies. Kretzmann and McKnight are the founders of this school of thought, and their 1993 book describes the principles and tools for applying this principle to high-poverty communities. Block's (2008) book discusses asset-based community, and presents concepts and approaches that can be translatable and effectively applied in higher education settings. Finally, Biswas-Diener's (2011) edited book presents a rich exploration of the merits of positive psychology in addressing issues of poverty and other forms of oppression.

Biswas-Diener, R. (ed.). *Positive Psychology as Social Change*. New York: Springer, 2011.

Block, P. *Community: The Structure of Belonging*. San Francisco: Berrett-Koehler, 2010.

Kretzmann, J. P., and McKnight, J. L. *Building Communities From the Inside Out: A Path Toward Finding and Mobilizing a Community's Assets*. Skokie, Ill.: ACTA Publications, 1993.

Journals

While positive psychology findings are being published in a wide variety of academic journals, these journals are specifically devoted to positive psychology or appreciative education.

Journal of Appreciative Education (http://libjournal.uncg.edu/index.php/jae/index)

Journal of Positive Psychology (http://www.tandfonline.com/loi/rpos20#. UgOR3hbkhSU)

Journal of Happiness Studies (http://www.springer.com/social+sciences/ wellbeing+%26+quality-of-life/journal/10902)

PETER C. MATHER *is an associate professor of Higher Education and Student Affairs and secretary to the board of trustees at Ohio University.*

EILEEN HULME *is the executive director of the Noel Academy for Strengths-Based Leadership and Education and a professor in the Department of Doctoral Higher Education at Azusa Pacific University.*

NEW DIRECTIONS FOR STUDENT SERVICES • DOI: 10.1002/ss

INDEX

95